ARCO

**Literary Critiques**

# Robert Browning

## Ioan M. Williams

arco

New York

# Acknowledgements

The author and publishers are indebted to the following for permission to use illustrations: The National Portrait Gallery for the painting by Field Talfourd which forms the cover, The Mansell Collection for the photograph of Browning as an older man and for the caricature of the meeting of the Browning Society by Max Beerbohm, Sir John Murray and the British Museum for the reproduction of a letter from Browning to G. Kingsland.

In addition, the quotation from *Hurry on Down* by John Wain has been used by kind permission of Martin Secker and Warburg Limited and the Viking Press, USA, and the lines from *Burnt Norton* in the *Four Quartets* by T. S. Eliot by permission of Faber and Faber Limited and Harcourt, Brace and World Incorporated.

Published 1970 by ARCO PUBLISHING COMPANY, Inc.
219 Park Avenue South, New York, N.Y. 10003
Copyright © Ioan M. Williams, 1967, 1970
All Rights Reserved
Library of Congress Catalog Number 70-101772
Printed in the United States of America

# Arco Literary Critiques

Of recent years, the ordinary man who reads for pleasure has been gradually excluded from that great debate in which every intelligent reader of the classics takes part. There are two reasons for this: first, so much criticism floods from the world's presses that no one but a scholar living entirely among books can hope to read it all; and second, the critics and analysts, mostly academics, use a language that only their fellows in the same discipline can understand.

Consequently criticism, which should be as 'inevitable as breathing'—an activity for which we are all qualified—has become the private field of a few warring factions who shout their unintelligible battle cries to each other but make little communication to the common man.

*Arco Literary Critiques* aims at giving a straightforward account of literature and of writers—straightforward both in content and in language. Critical jargon is as far as possible avoided; any terms that must be used are explained simply; and the constant preoccupation of the authors of the Series is to be lucid.

It is our hope that each book will be easily understood, that it will adequately describe its subject without pretentiousness so that the intelligent reader who wants to know about Donne or Keats or Shakespeare will find enough in it to bring him up to date on critical estimates.

Even those who are well read, we believe, can benefit from a lucid exposition of what they may have taken for granted, and perhaps—dare it be said?—not fully understood.

K. H. G.

# Browning

In 1891 Oscar Wilde wrote:

> Yes, Browning was great. And as what will he be remembered?
> As a poet? Ah, not as a poet!
>
> THE CRITIC AS ARTIST

This remark turned out to be more true than Wilde would have wanted it to be. For many years after his death Browning was remembered as a great teacher, an apostle of faith, the lover of Elizabeth Barrett—as anything but the author of a number of poems which have always been read and probably always will be. His contemporaries complained at first of the obscurity of his poetry and later grubbed in it for the wisdom which it was supposed to contain. As his ideas became unpopular and the reaction against Victorian idealism set in, his poetry became the object of critical attack because it put forward what was alleged to be a crude and immature ideology. In the last few years there has been a reaction from this unsympathetic attitude and Browning has begun to be considered not as a thinker whose thought is out of date, but as a poet. Critics are beginning again to examine and to confirm the quality of his work. It will never again be looked at as sympathetically as it was at the end of the nineteenth century, when it could be regarded as a kind of handbook to life. No modern reader can escape the conclusion that there are a large number of poems which he would not greatly miss from the body of Browning's work. Yet there are many which he will return to again and again, and it is because of these that the life and thought of Browning is of interest. To enable the reader to put these poems in perspective is the purpose of the present volume.

Quotations from the shorter poems and the plays of Browning are taken from the text published by Oxford University Press, 1957, except that from *Parleyings with Certain People*, for which the Smith Elder edition of 1889 was used. Quotations from *The Ring and the Book* are taken from the Oxford Edition, edited by Edward Dowden, 1912.     I. M. W.

4

# Contents

# The Author

Ioan M. Williams, is Lecturer in English
at the University of Warwick

Robert Browning in later life

I can have little doubt but that my writing has been, in the main, too hard for many I should have been pleased to communicate with: but I never designedly tried to puzzle people, as some of my critics have supposed. On the other hand, I never pretended to offer such literature as should be a substitute for a cigar, or game at dominoes to an idle man. So, perhaps on the whole I get my deserts and something over;— not a crowd but a few I value more. Let me see:

A letter from Robert Browning to his friend G. Kingsland, a painter

Robert Browning at a meeting of the Browning Society
by Max Beerbohm

# I

# Beginnings

John Wain, in his novel, *Hurry on Down*, describes a character called Froulish, a would-be novelist and cheerful exhibitionist:

> From early adolescence he had seen himself as the boy who, though as yet undistinguished in the eyes of the world, would reveal himself in due season as a great novelist. His whole life was lived in the pages of that monumental biography which was to be written, after his death, by some short-sighted silver-haired professor: ... Pope had been expelled from his first school for writing a satire on the master, Southey for declaring himself opposed to corporal punishment; Tennyson lived in thousands of hearts as the wild-eyed boy crouching in a deserted quarry and staring, long and incredulously, at the stone on which he had scratched the words 'Byron is dead'. Film! Pure film!
>
> HURRY ON DOWN CH. 2

Unlike Pope, Southey and Tennyson, Browning did nothing during his boyhood to provide his biographer with a central episode; the only part of his life which Hollywood has proved to be pure film is the courtship of Elizabeth Barrett. Unlike Froulish he did everything he could to prevent the discovery of any particularly significant facts about his boyhood and youth.

Browning was born in 1812 and lived quietly with his parents, first in Camberwell, and then, from 1840, at New Cross. His formal education was more or less complete by the time he was fourteen; he attended no public school or university, except for a short time at the newly established London University in 1828. Unlike most of the writers of the nineteenth century, he

9

never had to work for his living. Matthew Arnold and Arthur Clough worked in the Education Office and Anthony Trollope in the Post Office; Charles Lever acted as Consul at Spezia and Trieste; George Meredith, Charles Dickens and William Thackeray spent a good part of their youth as journalists. Browning never had to enter into any commitment which hindered his literary development. Instead, he was encouraged by an indulgent father to make use of an extensive library and to develop the faculty for verse-making which he had shown from the time that he could read. In later years he was extremely diligent and successful in preventing any of his early attempts from coming to light. Like her future husband, Elizabeth Barrett began writing at an early age. She wrote and published an epic poem on the battle of Marathon when she was fourteen, but made no attempt to suppress it when she came to maturity. Browning produced a manuscript volume of poems at roughly the same age, but he destroyed it a short time after its composition and did his best to make sure that no copy remained.

The little that we know about this volume is owing to the efforts of the person to whom it was presented and who seems to have been, at least in part, its inspiration. When he was thirteen, Browning met the sisters Sarah and Eliza Flower. They were the daughters of Benjamin Flower, ex-editor of the *Cambridge Intelligencer*, who had been imprisoned for his political opinions by the government of the Younger Pitt. When Browning met them, Eliza and Sarah were respectively nine and seven years older than him and were by all accounts intelligent, imaginative and beautiful. Eliza composed music and gained some reputation for herself as a writer of hymns; Sarah wrote poetry. To Eliza, Browning sent his volume, entitled *Incondita*. The account he gave of the matter in later years is typical of the way in which he persistently referred to his youthful productions. In a letter to Richard Hengest Horne, author of the epic poem, *Orion*, he said—

> . . . at twelve or thirteen, I wrote a book of verses which Eliza read and wrote to me about,—I wrote back,—then came the

acquaintance with Fox, if meeting him one evening be worth that name,—but she gave me his opinions at second hand, and more letters came of it: then in a few months (for one grows fast at that age) I saw the proper way, and put my blessed 'poems' in the fire. I lost (soon after) sight of Eliza,—but when, years after I began again, and printed a little thing, 'Pauline',— I could not but send it to Fox, my old praiser—thence fresh generosity from him, and reacquaintance with the Flowers, and one day Eliza told me to my amazement and discomfort that she had 'still by her somewhere, safe', all the letters I had written to her—'never being used to destroy a scrap of any such thing'—moreover producing on some occasion or other, a sort of album-book in which were entered 'poem' this and 'poem' the other, duly transcribed from my delectable collection aforesaid. 'I grinned and bore it.' . . .

After the death of Eliza, Browning obtained and destroyed this evidence of his youth. It is only by chance that we have a letter from Eliza Flower to William Johnson Fox, written in 1827, in which she copied two of the poems from the collection. The first of these, entitled *The First-Born of Egypt*, consists of eighty-three lines of blank verse and is close in tone to the verse dramas of Byron and Southey. It contains several lines justly marked out by the copyist:

> I marked one old man with his only son
> Lifeless within his arms—his withered hand
> Wandering o'er the features of his child
> Bidding him wake from that long dreary sleep,
> And lead his old blind father from the crowd
> To the green meadows . . .

The second poem, *The Dance of Death*, is made up of five speeches, given to Fever, Pestilence, Ague, Madness and Consumption, who claim in turn precedence as destructive forces. It is strongly indebted to a poem by Samuel Taylor Coleridge, entitled *Fire, Famine and Slaughter*. A fair example of the couplets in which it is composed is provided by the opening lines of the speech of Consumption:

'Tis for me, 'tis for me;
Mine the prize of Death must be;
My spirit is o'er the young and gay
As on snowy wreaths in the bright noonday
They wear a melting and vermeille flush
E'en while I bid their pulses hush . . .

THE DANCE OF DEATH

These poems are interesting for several reasons. They are the only indication that we have as to the way in which Browning was writing before his first publication, *Pauline*. They suggest that his reading up to this time was mainly in the work of Coleridge, Byron and Southey, rather than Shelley, who was later to be so important to him. What is most noticeable is that they are not autobiographical or personal in any way. This suggests that Browning adopted the first-person form for *Pauline* for dramatic reasons rather than because the poem was literally a confession of his own state of mind. Unless one realizes this, it is difficult to remember that what he says in that poem about the need for faith in an ideal beyond the self and the importance of human love as an indication of Divine Love is an early form of the statement which he was to go on making throughout his career.

'PAULINE'

*Pauline,* whose publication in 1833 was financed by the poet's aunt, is Browning's first published work. One of the most striking things about it is the degree to which it shows a very strong influence from the work of Shelley. The form of the poem is partly an imitation of Shelley's *Alastor,* or *The Spirit of Solitude,* and the speaker in *Pauline* attributes to the earlier poet a major part in his own development. The hero of the poem is himself a poet and to a considerable extent the personal experience which he describes seems to have been that of Browning himself. The material of the poem is the confession of the hero's spiritual biography during the most formative period of his life and his eventual salvation as a result of the beauty and virtue of the silent heroine, to whom the poem is addressed and after whom it is named. Browning went through just such a crisis— a crisis that seems partly to have been the result of a reading of the anti-Christian writings of Shelley. Browning seems to have come across Shelley's poems first in the pirated edition published by Benbow in 1826, just after the writing of *Incondita*. It appears, from a letter which Browning wrote to T. J. Wise in 1886, that he obtained the rest of Shelley's works very soon afterwards. Their impact on him was immediate and striking. Mrs. Orr, Browning's first biographer and personal friend, reported that he was for two years at this time a vegetarian, and for some time an atheist. Mrs. Orr also said that Browning's mother was very distressed by this phase in her son's development.

His mother's reaction to his intellectual rebellion was probably one of the major factors in Browning's return to faith. The poet always had a good relationship with his father. The elder Browning had been very harshly treated by his own father. He had returned from the family plantations in the Indies, after what seems to have been a particularly unpleasant experience of slavery, and had incurred his father's animosity. Consequently the elder Robert Browning had been obliged to seek uncongenial employment as a clerk in the Bank of England. He was evidently determined that *his* son should have all the opportunities of which he had been deprived. The result was encouragement from the father and grateful affection on the part of the son; Browning spoke with kindness and respect of his father until his death. On the other hand, his relationship with his mother seems to have been far more important to him emotionally. An indication of the extent to which he was involved with her is provided by the severity of his grief when she died in 1849, a week after the birth of his own son. Of her character we know little, but she was a very religious woman and we can imagine with what horror she would have reacted to signs of irreligion in her son. The intense affection which he felt for her suggests that intellectual rebellion would have soon seemed to him, as to her, a reason for guilt and shame.

The speaker in *Pauline* also suffered from confused feelings of guilt. The poem consists of a long monologue, punctuated by lyric passages, in which the speaker tells the woman who loves him about the history of his soul. The hero tells of an early loss of youthful idealism and sense of purpose, of his intellectual pride and the bitterness and emptiness which it brought him. He attributes all his spiritual troubles to the highly developed sense of 'self' which seems to possess him:

> I am made up of an intensest life,
> Of a most clear idea of consciousness
> Of self, distinct from all its qualities,
> From all affections, passions, feelings, powers;
> And thus far it exists, if tracked, in all:
> But linked, in me, to self-supremacy,
> Existing as a centre to all things,
> Most potent to create and rule and call
> Upon all things to minister to it;
> And to a principle of restlessness
> Which would be all, have, see, know, taste, feel, all . . .

An early and passionate enthusiasm for poetry, and particularly the poetry of Shelley, an eager devotion to the cause of humanity, and even a desire for fame—all these had disintegrated under the pressure of his sense of identity and self-absorption. Contact with the trustfulness and love of Pauline was necessary before he could recover from the hollow despair which had followed the period of pride and cynicism. Gradually, under her influence, he grew to understand that his rejection of early ideals had left nothing on which his 'restlessness of passion' and craving after knowledge could exercise themselves, and he turned once more towards God, whose nature had been suggested by the half-stifled yearnings of his own soul:

> Can I forgo the trust that he loves me?
> Do I not feel a love which only ONE . . .
> O thou pale form, so dimly seen, deep-eyed!
> I have denied thee calmly . . .

If I am erring save me, madden me,
Take from me powers and pleasures, let me die
Ages, so I see thee!

He intends to take the innocence and beauty of Pauline as immediate reminders of Divine Truth. Her love is to be an indication of the infinite possibilities of God's love. She will save him from the effects of his own intellect and over-consciousness of self:

We will go hand in hand,
I with thee, even as a child—love's slave,
Looking no farther than his liege commands.

The poem ends with an invocation to Shelley—'the Suntreader' —who is for the speaker the symbol of the poet's striving towards God by means of Truth and Love (the human ideals and the attributes of God).

INFLUENCE OF SHELLEY

This attitude to Shelley might seem rather surprising. The scepticism of the elder poet was partly responsible for the intellectual rebellion of the younger poet. *Pauline* represents a repudiation on the part of the author of the phase in his own life in which the work of Shelley was most influential. Because of this we might expect that Browning's poem would show some kind of a reaction from Shelley. Why it does not and why Browning's respect for Shelley persisted throughout the greater part of his life is revealed in the essay on the earlier poet which Browning wrote in 1852. The volume of letters, to which the essay was designed to form an introduction, was discovered shortly after its publication to be mainly composed of forgeries, but it was later republished with another collection of genuine letters. The essay shows that Browning centred on Shelley a group of ideas about the poet and his function which were of basic importance to him throughout his life. He describes what he calls 'the noblest and predominating characteristic of Shelley which places him in the ranks of the great writers':

This I call his simultaneous perception of Power and Love in the absolute, and of Beauty and Good in the concrete, while he throws, from his poet's station between both, swifter, subtler, and more numerous films for the connection of each with each, than have been thrown by any modern artificer of whom I have knowledge; proving how, as he says,

> The spirit of the worm within the sod,
> In love and worship blends itself with God.

I would rather consider Shelley's poetry as a sublime fragmentary essay towards a presentment of the correspondency of the universe to Deity, of the natural to the spiritual, and of the actual to the ideal, than I would isolate and separably appraise the worth of many detachable portions. . . .

ESSAY ON SHELLEY

The passage provides adequate explanation of the respect with which Shelley is treated in *Pauline*. He was for Browning the type of the poet, the imaginative soul who could see the relationship between the human and the Divine, between conditions in Time and conditions in Eternity. The distinction which he makes in the passage between the absolute and the concrete suggests his own struggle to conceive of the former and to give it concrete embodiment. In this attempt—or at least in his preoccupation with the disparity between the absolute and the relative, the ideal and the real—he had much in common with the majority of poets and thinkers of his age. To reconcile the sordidness of life with the brightness of spiritual conception was one of the major tasks of the Victorian writer. The same struggle for the absolute or the ideal was the task of several of the Romantic poets, and it was from their work that the thoughts of the Victorian writers developed. The high estimate which Coleridge, and after him Shelley, made of the function of the poet—the insistence on his creative powers and the fact that in exercising them he reflected the act of God in creating the world —was a major influence on Arnold, Clough, Patmore and Tennyson, as well as Browning. The insistence on the value of the imaginative powers as distinct from the intellectual ones— which was so great a feature of the work of Wordsworth and Keats—was a formative influence on the thought of many of the prose writers of the nineteenth century, on writers as far apart in intellectual inclination as the rationalist John Stuart Mill and the Catholic convert John Henry, Cardinal Newman. One of the major differences between the earlier writers and the later is the fact that the latter seem in their work to have lost confidence in the possibility of the reconciliation of the opposites, the real and the ideal, the imaginative and the intellectual. As the century wore on, some of them assumed defeat before they began, and retreated into aestheticism, or the doctrine that art has no purpose apart from being beautiful, so that William Morris could write in the Apology which prefaced his *Earthly Paradise* in 1868:

> Dreamer of dreams, born out of my due time,
> Why should I strive to set the crooked straight?
> Let it suffice me that my murmuring rhyme
> Beats with light wing against the ivory gate,
> Telling a tale not too importunate
> To those who in the sleepy region stay,
> Lulled by the singer of an empty day.

In this poem Morris rejects the idea that literature is in any way meaningful; to him it is merely a pleasant way of escaping from the boredom of contemporary England. Many writers who did not take this course kept, like Matthew Arnold, their high estimate of the function of the poet, but thought of poetry more in terms of Beauty, losing, as a result, the immediacy and impact which comes from a concern with the concrete situation. Browning and Arthur Clough were among the few exceptions. Both avoided the tendency to think of poetry primarily in terms of Beauty—and consequently in terms of word music and ornamentation—rather than meaning.

*Pauline* was the nearest Browning ever approached to this type of poetry—the type of which Tennyson was the main exemplar. The rest of his career shows a development farther and farther away from it. Yet, as I have already said, it is important to realize that the thought which lies behind the poem is in essentials that which is contained in his very latest work. When the poem first came out, a review copy was sent by Fox to John Stuart Mill. Mill did not actually review the poem, but, under the impression that he was to do so, he wrote his comments in the margins and fly-leaf of the book. His criticism was harsh. While he spoke highly of the quality of certain lines and passages, his assessment of the tone of the work was scathing. His comment began:

> With considerable poetic power, this writer seems to me possessed with a more intense and morbid self-consciousness than I ever knew in any sane human being. . . .

and ended:

> Meanwhile he should not attempt to show how a person may be *recovered* from this morbid state—for *he* is hardly convalescent, and 'what should we speak of but that which we know?'

The volume containing this criticism found its way back to the poet. It is still in existence, including not only Mill's comments, but Browning's answers to them. It is often asserted that this was a fact of major importance in Browning's career. Certain critics see the formal development in Browning's work, the movement away from poetry which appears subjective or autobiographical, as the result of Browning's reaction to Mill's severity. In fact, there is no evidence to suggest that Browning's reaction was at all violent. Moreover, there is every reason to believe that, while the experience described in *Pauline* was to some extent the experience of the young poet, he saw the poem far more objectively than we sometimes assume. In his later essay on Shelley he spoke of two types of poet, the subjective and the objective. He defined them as follows:

> . . . the objective poet, in his appeal to the aggregate human mind, chooses to deal with the doings of men (the result of which dealing, in its pure form, when even description, as

suggesting a describer, is dispensed with, is what we call dramatic poetry), while the subjective poet, whose study has been himself, appealing through himself to the absolute Divine mind, prefers to dwell upon those external scenic appearances which strike out most abundantly and uninterruptedly his inner light and power. . . .

ESSAY ON SHELLEY

According to this definition, much of *Pauline* is the work of the subjective poet, who gives in his description of things outside himself a reflection of his own soul. On the other hand, Browning's remark about the poem, in a pencilled note, suggests that he was also thinking of himself as an objective poet:

> The following Poem was written in pursuance of a foolish plan which occupied me mightily for a time, and which had for its object the enabling me to assume and realize I know not how many different characters: meanwhile the world was never to guess that 'Brown, Smith, Jones, and Robinson' (as the spelling books have it) the respective authors of this poem, the other novel, such an opera, such a speech etc etc were no other than one and the same individual. The present abortion was the first work of the *Poet* of the batch, who would have been more legitimately *myself* than most of the others; but I surrounded him with all manner of (to my then notion) poetical accessories, and had planned quite a delightful life for him.
>
> Only this crab remains of the shapely Tree of Life in this Fool's Paradise of mine.

His original intention seems to have included the writing of both objective and subjective poetry.

The phrase in the passage which refers to *Pauline* as the work of the poet who 'would have been more legitimately myself than most of the others', refers not so much to any autobiographical aspect of the poem, as to what Browning meant when he wrote to Elizabeth Barrett that his ambition was to create, 'R[obert] B[rowning], a poem'. Throughout his career he thought of his work as a manifestation of his personality. In fact, he seems to have spent his life in the attempt to

19

contain within himself the two types of poet about whom he spoke in the essay on Shelley—to be both an objective and a subjective poet. It is important that already, when he was writing *Pauline,* he was thinking in terms of this task.

## 'PARACELSUS'

It was the publication of *Paracelsus* which first brought Browning literary fame. In 1834 he had been thinking of a career in diplomacy. He had visited Russia in the suite of the Russian Consul General, De Benkhausen, between March and May 1834. He was also friendly at this time with an agent of the French Royalists, Amédée de Ripert-Monclar. It was he who suggested to Browning the subject of his new poem. He had already begun to work on *Sordello,* the poem which was eventually published in March 1840, but he took up the subject of the life of Paracelsus, the famous sixteenth-century Swiss physician and philosopher, with enthusiasm, and wrote the poem during the last four months of 1834 and the first two of 1835.

The form of the poem is superficially that of a drama, but as Browning points out in the preface, it is in fact a poem:

> I am anxious that the reader should not . . . judge it by principles on which it was never moulded, and subject it to standards to which it was never meant to conform. . . . It is an attempt, probably more novel than happy, to reverse the method usually adopted by writers whose aim it is to set forth any phenomenon of the mind or the passions, by the operation of persons and events; and that, instead of having recourse to an external machinery of incidents to create and evolve the crisis I desire to produce, I have ventured to display somewhat minutely the mood itself in its rise and progress. . . .

The poem is divided into five sections, each consisting of dialogue between Paracelsus, his friends Festus and Michal, or the poet Aprile. The poem contains no action. Although each of the sections relates to a period in the life of the main character, Paracelsus, the real subject matter is not so much his life as the history of his mental development. We follow him throughout his search for the Absolute. He seeks to understand God and the Universe, firstly through obtaining Knowledge and later by means of Love. His life is a dismal tale of superb aspiration and utter failure, until, at the end, he does perceive the truth about the relationship between God and Man. On his death-bed he understands that Man's true task is not to seek for abstract Truth, but to follow out the divine elements in his own nature and thus to evolve himself into a higher being, approaching closer to God.

## Part 1. Paracelsus Aspires

The first scene is set in a garden at Würtzburg where Michal and Festus, the friends of Paracelsus, attempt to dissuade him from his determination to devote his life to an attempt to obtain absolute Knowledge. Paracelsus has recognized the divine nature of Knowledge, a quality which can be attained in part by human beings and is possessed in full by God. Festus is disturbed not only by the thought of losing his friend, but also by the thought of possible dangers awaiting the soul of Paracelsus in such an audacious attempt. Consequently, he asks for proof that Paracelsus is right in making the attempt:

> Prove that to me—but that! Prove you abide
> Within their warrant, nor presumptuous boast
> God's labour laid on you; prove, all you covet
> A mortal may expect; and, most of all,
> Prove the strange course you now affect, will lead
> To its attainment. . . .

What disturbs Festus most deeply is the thought that, even if the aim of his friend is right, the means may be wrong. If Paracelsus is correct in assuming that God wishes man to strive to attain the Absolute, is he also right in sacrificing his whole life to the attempt? Paracelsus replies by stating that the spirit within him which gave him his aim—

> Which sought to comprehend the works of God,
> And God himself, and all God's intercourse
> With the human mind. . . .

—also dictates the means by which this aim must be achieved. This spirit tells him that nothing short of complete dedication of the whole self to the desired end will make the achievement possible. All his human desires and weaknesses must be repressed in order to allow him to go straight forward to the goal of Knowledge.

Festus is overcome in argument, but unconvinced. He is disturbed by Paracelsus's determination to deny himself any enjoyment of human love. His friend states a doctrine in reply which is basic in Browning's thought—that Man should struggle to refine those elements of the divine which lie hidden within himself:

> ... to KNOW
> Rather consists in opening out a way
> Whence the imprisoned splendour may escape,
> Than in effecting entry for a light
> Supposed to be without.

He is convinced that human strength is sufficient for his search, and the scene ends with an assertion of faith in him by Festus and Michal. Yet the warning of Festus about the danger of ignoring human love is not to be forgotten; it is an indication of what is to be the major discovery of the hero in the next scene.

### Part 2. Paracelsus Attains

In this scene we see Paracelsus in the house of a Greek magician in Constantinople. Nine years have passed since he began the search. He has come to Constantinople in order to obtain the help of the Greek. A condition of receiving that help was that he should prepare an account of his career so far. The result of the review which he makes is the mood of disillusionment in which we find him at the beginning of the scene. His determination to rely on his human strength in order to attain his end has now begun to slacken. He seeks rest from his labour and some sense of reward for his nine years of absolute devotion to his task. So far, life itself has been sacrificed to the pursuit of the Absolute:

One vast unbroken chain of thought, kept up
Through a career apparently adverse
To its existence: life, death, light and shadow,
The shows of the world, were bare receptacles. . . .

Now, after he has long ignored his humanity, it has come in the form of weakness and premature agedness, to make him despair of the achievement of his purpose.

At this point Paracelsus is meditating on the ability of God to restore his worn-out youth—or in other words, to extend the capacity of his human nature so that he will be able to fulfil the task which he thinks God Himself has set him. Suddenly he hears a voice singing some way off. He soon discovers the voice to be that of the poet, Aprile. Aprile is in a state of semi-madness, on the verge of death. Just as Paracelsus sought for absolute Knowledge, Aprile sought for Love:

I would LOVE infinitely and be beloved!

Aprile has failed because he has ignored the means available to him for achieving this end. In speaking of Love he included all modes of creation; he wished to be a poet, painter, sculptor and musician. In creating, he thought to reveal the love within himself and to attract the love of other men towards himself:

Last, having thus revealed all I could love,
Having received all love bestowed on it,
I would die: preserving so throughout my course
God full on me, as I was full on men:
He would approve my prayer, 'I have gone through
'The loveliness of life; create for me
'If not for men, or take me to thyself,
'Eternal, infinite love!'

This account of his ambition reveals the fact that he has started from a point similar to that from which Paracelsus began. The difference between them is that one has conceived of God in terms of Knowledge, the other in terms of Love. Both have attempted to act the part of God to the full extent of their human capacities. Aprile has failed through too great a concern with the self.

It is important to realize that Aprile's idea of the poet is that held by Browning himself. One has only to examine the essay on Shelley to see that Browning is putting forward there much the same idea as that contained in the words of Aprile. The poet is a kind of middleman between God and Man, demonstrating to the latter what his true relationship with God should be. The same idea is grasped by Sordello, the hero of the poem which Browning had set aside to work on *Paracelsus*. It is obvious that during these years he was deeply concerned with the question of the exact nature of the poet's task. That Paracelsus himself is not a poet only indicates the fact that the responsibility of the poet is shared by all men, whatever their field of activity. Conversely, the failure of Aprile suggests also in what way Paracelsus is wrong.

Aprile's love of beauty, his desire to create, became self-indulgent. His inspiration led not to a sharing of his vision with mankind, but to a life spent in dreaming. Ironically he believes that Paracelsus, who *has* devoted himself to something outside his own existence, has succeeded. He dies in that belief, leaving Paracelsus with a new understanding of the path to God. The hero's words after Aprile's death reveal the meaning of the title of this section:

> Thy spirit, at least, Aprile! Let me love!
> I have attained, and now I may depart.

He has reached the perception which the less brilliant Festus made in the first scene. Knowledge alone is not enough. God is Love as well as being the power which Paracelsus sees as Knowledge.

*Part 3. Paracelsus*
This scene takes place after an interval of five years. Paracelsus is now famous as a teacher at the University of Basil (Basle).

Festus has recently rediscovered his friend whom he recognizes as the now famous doctor whose name is in every mouth. Festus insists on complimenting Paracelsus on his obvious success, moved by what he has heard about the enthusiasm of his friend's pupils. As the scene proceeds, Paracelsus gradually reveals to Festus the irony of this praise. He is bitter and disillusioned. Moved by the discovery of Love to which Aprile had brought him, he had decided to devote his learning to the service of his fellow men. Having tried to do so, he was forced even in his apparent success, to realize that he was surrounded by ignorance and stupidity. He tells Festus:

> . . . you know my hopes;
> I am assured, at length, those hopes were vain;
> The truth is just as far from me as ever;
> That I have thrown my life away. . . .

In his bitterness he explains to Festus that the only course now open to him is to endure in the attempt to teach until he meets with the rejection which he already foresees. He cannot change the nature of his soul as his life has moulded it. He must persist in the course which he has marked out for himself, even with the consciousness of failure.

Festus attempts to persuade his friend to commit his knowledge to the press, so that what cannot be appreciated by the present generation can be saved for those to come. But Paracelsus explains that the full extent of his knowledge is a few simple principles and incidental secrets of nature—some few hints of a vast design. They will be as useful now as in the future:

> For if mankind intend to learn at all,
> They must begin by giving faith to them
> And acting on them. . . .

Nothing Festus says can remove his conviction that his search has brought nothing but unhappiness and made him fit for no other course of life. He ends the scene by giving expression to the fear which Festus had previously conceived:

> Love, hope, fear, faith—these make humanity;
> These are its sign and note and character,
> And these I have lost!

All Festus can obtain is a promise that when he is in trouble he will call on his friend.

### Part 4. Paracelsus Aspires

The scene is now set in Alsatia, two years later. Driven from Basil with scorn, Paracelsus has turned to wine as a source of strength in his degradation. He still seeks to know; but he is now attempting to escape from the fear of sacrificing himself to no end by indulging his senses:

> I seek to know and to enjoy at once,
> Not one without the other as before.
> Suppose my labour should seem God's own cause
> Once more, as first I dreamed,—it shall not baulk me
> Of the meanest earthliest sensualest delight
> That may be snatched; for every joy is gain,
> And gain is gain, however small.

In answer to Festus's exhortation that he assume a new austerity of purpose and escape from his abasement, Paracelsus sings a song. The song is an account of other seekers after Truth who reached what they thought was the true end of their journey, only to find, too late, that they had stopped too soon. Like them, he is incapable of making a new start. The discovery that Michal, the wife of Festus, and his early friend, is now dead, only serves to confirm him in his conviction that it is too late for a new beginning.

This scene, and especially the song which Paracelsus sings, shows the hero possessed by a kind of melancholy resignation which is a common strain in Victorian literature. William Morris's *Earthly Paradise* is the story of a group of adventurers doomed to fail in their search for an unattainable ideal. The poetry of Matthew Arnold is impregnated with a similar sense of the futility of action. His Empedocles, in *Empedocles on Etna*, is

26

overcome by a sense of the disparity between the Ideal and the Real. The same feeling receives morbid analysis in James Thompson's *City of Dreadful Night,* and pervades the poetry of Dante Gabriel Rossetti. A poem from his sonnet sequence, *The House of Life,* illustrates the mood of elegant despair:

> Think thou and act; tomorrow thou shalt die.
>> Outstretched in the sun's warmth upon the shore,
>> Thou say'st: 'Man's measured path is all gone o'er:
> Up all his years, steeply, with strain and sigh,
> Man clomb until he touched the truth; and I,
>> Even I, am he whom it was destined for.'
>> How should this be? Art thou then so much more
> Than they who sowed, that thou shouldst reap thereby?
>
> Nay, come up hither. From this wave-washed mound
>> Unto the furthest flood-brim look with me;
> Then reach on with thy thought till it be drown'd.
>> Miles and miles distant though the last line be,
> And though thy soul sail leagues and leagues beyond,—
>> Still, leagues beyond those leagues, there is more sea.
>
> THE CHOICE

The feeling which this sonnet produces is one which leads away from any positive action rather than towards it, as does the song in this part of *Paracelsus*. It is a feeling which many of the Victorian poets never tired of expressing. At best it results in the mournful beauty of some of the poetry of Arnold and Morris or in the *Morte d'Arthur* of Tennyson; at worst, it results in nothing but morbid sentimentality.

The use of the song in *Paracelsus* shows the extent to which Browning had developed since he wrote *Pauline*. In the earlier poem, because there is no distinction between author and speaker, we are left with the same feeling of nostalgia at lost innocence and lost opportunity. But Paracelsus goes farther in his development than the hero of *Pauline*. Browning's later hero has another phase of development to pass through until, at the end of the poem, he achieves the truth which he has spent his life in seeking.

## Part 5. Paracelsus Attains

This last scene takes place in a hospital in Salzburg, thirteen years later. Paracelsus is dying. Festus is sitting by his bedside, listening to his delirium. Festus prays that God should save Paracelsus's soul, urging that his sincerity and nobleness amply compensate for his departure from the course which God had laid out for all men to follow. After this prayer we hear the ravings of the semi-conscious Paracelsus, reliving his life and failure; in his delirium he is with the dead poet Aprile:

> Where are we put, Aprile?
> Have they left us in the lurch? This murky loathsome
> Death-trap, this slaughter-house, is not the hall
> In the golden city! Keep by me, Aprile!
> There is a hand groping amid the blackness
> To catch us.

His mind wanders through a mixture of fantasy and reality, catching in desperation at conflicting explanations of his failure. Eventually he returns to consciousness and recognizes his old friend. Now, for the first time, he finds consolation in the fact that he is human, and therefore weak. In death he wishes to join his fellow human beings:

> . . . dear Festus, lay me,
> When I shall die, within some narrow grave . .
> . . . lay me thus, then say, 'He lived
> 'Too much advanced before his brother men;
> 'They kept him still in front: 'twas for their good
> 'But yet a dangerous station. It were strange
> 'That he should tell God he had never ranked
> 'With men: so, here at least he is a man.'

Towards the end, as Festus sings to him of the beauty which surrounded them in their youth, he begins to understand the mystery of life as he has never done before. He rises from his bed, dresses himself as in the days of his success at Basil, and declares that he is happy and resigned to the course of his life.

For the first time he sees his life in perspective and understands that real happiness came to him only when he 'vowed himself to Man'. With renewed conviction that the task of him who would aspire is to draw out the divine elements in his human nature, he makes a statement which is central to Browning's thought and which marks the climax of the poem. The attributes of God are:

> Convergent in the faculties of man.
> Power—neither put forth blindly, nor controlled
> Calmly by perfect knowledge; to be used
> At risk, inspired or checked by hope and fear:
> Knowledge—not intuition, but the slow
> Uncertain fruit of an enhancing toil,
> Strenthened by love: love—not serenely pure,
> But strong from weakness. . . .

This is the full vision of Man as it comes to Paracelsus. Man has within him, as has all creation, the attributes of his Creator—Power, Knowledge and Love. Because they are not pure, as they are in God, it is the task of Man to refine them and make himself more like God. He must live according to these divine principles within him.

Before he dies, Paracelsus knows that mankind must begin from the vision of its own capacity for perfection. When Man has perfected himself, then a new process will begin:

> . . . in completed man begins anew
> A tendency to God.

This knowledge comes to him with the knowledge of where he failed and why he failed. Looking back over the course of his life he sees that until he met Aprile he could see only one of the divine attributes:

> Power; I could not take my eyes from that:
> That only, I thought, should be preserved, increased
> At any risk, displayed, struck out at once—
> The sign and note and character of man.

He had learnt from Aprile 'the worth of love in Man's estate', but he had failed to regard his fellow men in terms of that love. He had failed to realize that love, as an essential part of his own nature, should have been directed towards mankind:

> In my own heart love had not been made wise
> To trace love's faint beginnings in mankind,
> To know even hate is but a mask of love's,
> To see a good in evil, and a hope
> In ill-success. . . .

His last visionary hope is that future generations will be able to succeed where he had failed—that they will be able to unite the scattered elements of the divine, to see the relationship of Power and Love, and live by exercising Power in terms of Love.

### 'SORDELLO'

*Sordello* was eventually published in March 1840, after seven years of intermittent work. The result of the publication was the temporary destruction of the literary reputation which had begun to come to Browning after the publication of *Paracelsus*. At this time in his life, when the favourable reception of *Paracelsus* had made his name known in London, he moved in the literary world, meeting men as well established in that world as Sergeant Talford, author of the poetic drama, *Ion*; Henry Horne, author of *Orion* and the collection of critical essays entitled *A New Spirit of the Age*; and William Wordsworth. It was at a dinner given to mark the success of *Ion* that Wordsworth complimented the younger poet, and Charles Macready, actor and theatre manager, asked Browning to write a play for him to perform. At the same time Browning was on intimate terms with John Forster, who was later to write the authoritative biography of Dickens. In 1838 he visited Italy for the first time, collecting information for *Sordello*. This must have been one of the pleasantest periods of Browning's life, with everything to hope for in terms of literary success and the enjoyment of its rewards already beginning. The publication of *Sordello* put an end to this period; the poem's reception made Browning's name synonymous with obscurity and confusion. It took several years and the increased clarity of the poems which he published in the *Bells and Pomegranates* series, to restore his reputation to the position at which it stood in 1839.

*Sordello* is not one of those poems which improve with time. The modern reader finds *Sordello* just as difficult to read and to understand as did Browning's contemporaries. Before it can be read at all it is necessary to have a clear idea of the political background against which the life of its hero is lived. The poem is set in northern Italy at the beginning of the thirteenth century. The political action described in it is part of the great struggle between the Guelphs—supporting the Pope—and the Ghibellines—supporting the Emperor—at the time when those two personages were struggling for political control in Europe. The action involved in the poem stretches from the youth of one of the main characters, Taurello Salinguerra, a Ghibelline leader, to his old age, capture and death, which occurs after about sixty years of intense activity and intrigue. The most important of the persons referred to in the poem are as follows:

*Guelphs*
Pope Honorius III
Azzo Este, head of the House of Este, leader of the Guelphs
Count Richard Boniface, Azzo's ally
Agnes Este, daughter of Azzo Este and first wife of Ecelin Romano
*Ghibellines*
Emperor Frederick II
Ecelin Romano, head of the Ghibellines
Taurello Salinguerra, warrior and main supporter of Ecelin
Palma, daughter of Ecelin by Agnes Este
Adelaide, wife of Ecelin after the death of Agnes
Ecelino and Alberic, sons of Ecelin
Sordello, a poet; believed to be the son of a Ghibelline archer, Elcorte, but actually the son of Salinguerra by his dead wife, Retrude.

Characters involved in the life of Sordello but not involved in the political action are Eglamor, a poet, and Naddo, a critic.

The poem actually begins when the poet Sordello is a man of some thirty years, but it moves through a very complex series of events which it is of the utmost importance to understand. These events began when the young Salinguerra, heir to the city of Vincenza in northern Italy, was deprived of his promised bride by Azzo Este. He fled to the Emperor and was rewarded with the hand of the latter's daughter, Retrude. He returned to northern Italy and made common cause with Ecelin Romano against the Guelph party led by Azzo. The most important event at this stage was the withdrawal, in the face of superior force, of Ecelin and Salinguerra from the city of Vincenza, during which they set fire to the quarter of the city inhabited by their enemies. In the resulting confusion and slaughter, Ecelin's wife, Adelaide, was delivered of a son; at the same time, Salinguerra's wife, Retrude, also bore a son. Both women were rescued by an insignificant archer, Elcorte, at the expense of his own life, but shortly afterwards Retrude died. Adelaide, afraid that Salinguerra's son would take precedence over her own, now pretended that the child was Elcorte's and brought it up as such in her own castle at Goito, near Mantua.

Salinguerra, under the impression that his child had died with his wife, lost any sense of personal ambition and spent his life fighting for the cause of Ecelin Romano. Together with Adelaide he supported the weak-willed Ecelin until, when he was away and Adelaide was recently dead, Ecelin made a sudden decision to leave the world and enter a monastery. Before doing so, he arranged for alliances between his children, Ecelino and Alberic, and members of the house of Azzo, and betrothed his daughter Palma to Count Richard Boniface.

Salinguerra rushed back when he heard the news but arrived too late to prevent Ecelin from carrying out his intention. He pretended acquiescence in the situation but intrigued for a breaking out of hostilities before the marriage of Palma and Boniface. He succeeded in achieving this and at the siege of

Ferrara captured Boniface. The capture was followed by a truce while the representatives of the Lombard League of Guelph cities sued for restoration of their leader.

Browning begins his poem at this point. Everything which happens before, including the youth of the hero, Sordello, is given in retrospect. The events which occur after this centre around Palma's attempt to persuade Sordello and Salinguerra to work together. The climax of the story is the revelation that Sordello is Salinguerra's son—a fact which Palma had learnt from Ecelin, to whom Adelaide confessed it on her deathbed. After this revelation there is a great temptation for Sordello. With renewed hope in life and the possibility of success, Salinguerra prophesies victory for the Ghibelline cause with himself and his son as its leaders. However, Sordello has recently come to the conviction that the Ghibelline cause is wrong; that the interests of the people, which he now sees as paramount, would be better served by a Guelph victory on behalf of the Pope. He has to struggle against the temptation to betray his conviction, and in surmounting it he dies. Browning concludes the poem by giving an account of the disintegration of the Ghibelline party after his death, telling of the fate of Ecelin and Alberic and depicting the aged and hopeless Salinguerra as a degenerate and ineffective bandit. He dies in captivity.

Like the hero and speaker of *Pauline*, and like Paracelsus, Sordello is a noble imaginative spirit. Like them, he is a failure in that he does not bring his own qualities to their proper fulfilment. It is only towards the end of his life that he makes the same realization that Paracelsus made—that Man's proper service is to his fellow men. Then it is too late because the self-indulgent life which he has lived has deprived him of even the little strength needed to bear the new understanding. In some senses Sordello is the soul to Salinguerra's body. He possessed the imaginative vision which was necessary to inform and direct the power of his father. Consequently it is appropriate that the poem goes on after his death and that we learn about the decline of Salinguerra.

The idea behind the poem is not complex; at any rate, no more complex than the idea behind *Paracelsus*. But *Sordello* is a very complex poem—so complex that few readers of Browning succeed in making sense of it at all. The main reason for this is in the way Browning connects the story of his hero to the action in which he is involved. Elizabeth Barrett twice found occasion to blame the construction of the poem as a source of difficulty. In September 1845 she wrote:

> [*Sordello*] wants drawing together and fortifying in the connections and associations . . . which hang as loosely every here and there, as those in a dream, and confound the reader who persists in thinking himself awake.

Then, in December of the same year:

> . . . 'Sordello' *deserves* the labour which it needs, to make it appear the great work it is. I think that the principle of association is too subtly in movement throughout it—so that *while* you are going straight forward you go at the same time round and round, until the progress involved in the motion is lost sight of by the lookers on.

This comment touches on the central fault of the poem. The principle which governs the sequence of events is nowhere visible to the reader; it is, in fact, the principle of association in the mind of the narrator. This might not be harmful in a poem which took the consciousness of the narrator as its focal point, any more than it is harmful in a first-person novel such as William Golding's *Free Fall*. However, in *Sordello*, we are only aware of the consciousness of the narrator at certain points. At others we are taken up with Sordello himself, with other characters, or with the historical events. The changes in sequence, which mean that the reader has, without reason given, suddenly to adjust himself to widely separated times and places, increase this difficulty without giving any advantage. These characteristics may be seen in the analysis of the structure and content of the poem which follows.

*Book 1*

After an invocation to an imaginary audience of dead poets and an appeal to contemporary readers, Browning gives a vivid description of the reaction of the people of Verona to the news that their leader, Count Richard Boniface, had been captured by Salinguerra. He then focuses on a single room in the city where Sordello and Palma are spending the night in urgent discussion. This glimpse is followed by an invocation to Dante, the great poetic successor to Sordello, who achieved much of what the earlier poet failed to achieve. When this is over Browning changes the time from the present, in which the mature Sordello talks with Palma, to the past, in order to describe the youth of the poet, which was spent in the castle at Goito, where Sordello was alone except for Adelaide, the infant Palma and his own fancies.

At this point Browning again interrupts the narrative to insert a passage which is of central importance both to the poem and to his own aesthetic doctrine. He says that there are two types of the imaginative or poetic temperament. He describes the first type as follows:

> One character
> Denotes them through the progress and the stir,—
> A need to blend with each external charm,
> Bury themselves, the whole heart wide and warm,—
> In something not themselves; they would belong
> To what they worship. . . .

The poet who is of this type is basically unconscious of his own individuality; the intensity of his perception of, and sympathy with, objects outside himself makes him submerge his personality in theirs.

The second type of temperament is basically self-conscious. A poet of this type identifies all things outside himself with himself. To this type of man anything outside himself, 'or good, or wise, or strong', is related to something within himself, and he remains conscious of himself all the time that he is conscious of the object. This second type can aspire to a higher form of life than is possible to the first; his self-consciousness can lead to a degree of self-cultivation which is impossible to the humbler person who never thinks of himself. On the other hand, the self-conscious type is subject to two great temptations: first, to be content with his own vision and not to strive to impart it to other men. Browning remarks of this second type:

> Ah, but to find
> A certain mood enervate such a mind,
> Counsel it slumber in the solitude
> Thus reached nor, stooping, task for mankind's good
> Its nature just as life and time accord. . . .

This was the temptation which destroyed Aprile, in *Paracelsus*.

The second temptation is even more dangerous. The self-conscious poet may escape the temptation to be too introverted, but even if he does, and determines on putting his vision of a higher life into reality, he may fall into the temptation of ignoring the limitations of human life and attempt to force his perceptions on the present time and the present conditions. He may, says Browning, attempt:

> . . . to display completely here
> The mastery another life should learn,
> Thrusting in time eternity's concern. . . .

To direct our reading of this passage and warn us that it contains a statement of the main theme of the poem, we have Browning's own words in a letter to his friend, Dowden, in March 1866:

> You are quite right about the classification of Sordello's—neither with the first nor the second of those moods of mind: it is the second as 'enervated' and modified by the impulse to 'thrust in time eternity's concern'—*that*, or nothing. This is just indicated in the passage where these words occur, and the rest of the poem is an example of the same.

From this passage we learn that Sordello was an example of the second type of temperament and that he had fallen into the second temptation which Browning mentions. We are also told that the whole poem is devoted to expressing this idea. After this passage in the poem we know that Sordello is in danger of falling into the temptation of ignoring the actual conditions of human life and human nature and trying to express his ideal conceptions in the present time.

After the discussion of the two types Browning goes on to describe Sordello's gradual awakening to self-consciousness and his desire to prove his own estimation of himself to the world. Having no conception of the life of men, he projects his imagination into the lives of princes and heroes. He fancies himself to be Apollo, God of Poetry, the type of beauty and power. Yet, in spite of his imagination, sometimes his visions fade and reality returns to disappoint him. The book ends with an account of his dissatisfaction with his inactive state and with a forewarning of an event which is to change the course of his life.

*Book 2*
This event occurs when Sordello stumbles upon a gathering of people at Mantua. At this gathering Palma and Adelaide are listening to Eglamor, a poet who is singing a lay in Palma's honour. Sordello listens, entranced by the beauty of Palma, whom he has imagined in his lonely dreams as his ideal love. He is impelled, by what seems to him to be the ineptitude of Eglamor's lay, to seize his lyre and re-tell the subject of the song. He sings so well that he wins the prize and receives it from Palma while Eglamor retires—to die of his disappointment. Sordello is borne by the crowd back to Goito. There he spends a week in wondering over what has happened to him, until he meets by chance with the corpse of Eglamor being borne to burial. The importance of the dead poet is that he is a foil to Sordello. Eglamor is an example of the first type of poet mentioned in Book 1, dedicated to his art and, though capable of only the lower flights of the imagination, loving beauty with no regard for his own self. In contrast with Eglamor the essential vanity and self-consciousness of Sordello is emphasized.

Sordello's self-esteem meets with a temporary rebuff when he discovers the supposed fact of his descent from the low-born archer Elcorte. This discovery puts an end to his dreams and fantasies about his origins and throws him back upon his own self and his actions. He had presumed himself of divine birth, playing the part of Apollo, and the recent victory in song had allowed him to think of himself as apart from other men, with no need to attempt to find material expression of his power:

> The world shall bow to me conceiving all
> Man's life, who see its blisses, great and small,
> Afar—not tasting any; no machine
> To exercise my utmost will is mine:
> Be mine mere consciousness! Let men perceive
> What I could do, a mastery believe,
> Asserted and established to the throng
> By their selected evidence of song. . . .

The machine he refers to in this passage is the medium of expressing his higher or mental life in the realm of matter—in other words, the body. Sordello decides to select the function of the poet as the only method of expressing his superiority over other men, standing aside both from bodily action and enjoyment. In this state of mind he accepts the invitation of Naddo to go to Mantua and exercise his new craft of poetry.

At first Sordello meets with nothing but success at Mantua, but gradually he becomes dissatisfied with the ordinary song, with the subject matter of human love and action. He attempts to create, through his song, an accurate representation of his own inner life and the working of his imagination. His attempt fails because he cannot adapt language to his new purpose:

> Because perceptions whole, like that he sought
> To clothe, reject so pure a work of thought
> As language: thought may take perception's place
> But hardly co-exist in any case,
> Being its mere presentment—of the whole
> By parts, the simultaneous and the sole
> By the successive and the many.

The ideas involved in this passage represent a drawing out of the distinction between thought and imagination which is found in the criticism of Coleridge and Keats. Both these writers make a distinction between the ordinary mode of thought, which depends on language for its formulation, and the kind of intuitive or imaginative perception which is apart from, and cannot be expressed in, language.

The idea of the poet's function which Sordello is attempting to put into practice is closely allied to that which is explained in Shelley's *A Defence of Poetry*, where he says that it is the exercise of the imagination which makes the advancement of thought possible.

What Sordello is attempting to do is, in Browning's opinion, the basic task of every poet. He meets the difficulty which every poet must meet. The language, which is his only mode of expression, is suitable for the expression of *thought* because both are *consecutive*. On the other hand, perception, the work of the *imagination*, is not consecutive, but instantaneous, and cannot be expressed in a medium which depends on the sequence of words. In order to avoid this difficulty, Sordello tortures the language, twisting word order and syntax—as did the Provençal poets in their fantastically complex patterns of metre and rhyme. In fact, what Sordello is trying to do is more or less what many modern poets have attempted to do, and something which Browning's contemporaries, Dante Gabriel Rossetti and Gerard Manley Hopkins, also attempted, though in very different ways. T. S. Eliot commented on this problem in his *Four Quartets*:

> Words move, music moves
> Only in time; but that which is only living
> Can only die. . . .
>        Only by the form, the pattern,
> Can words or music reach
> The stillness. . . .

BURNT NORTON 5, *137–142*

Eliot's 'stillness' is roughly equivalent to Browning's 'simultaneous and the sole'. Dante Gabriel Rossetti implied what

Eliot states in *Burnt Norton*, when he called a sonnet a 'moment's monument'. Gerard Manley Hopkins, in poems like *The Windhover*, also tried to escape from the sequential nature of language. Unlike Sordello, however, Hopkins wrote about a bird rather than a 'perception'. He succeeded.

Inevitably Sordello fails, and his poems are unpopular. His audience, accustomed to conventional verse, demand that he recount stories in his songs. When he does so, they fail to see beyond the greatness of the actions which he celebrates, to the greatness of the poet himself. Consequently he becomes disillusioned and divided between the desire to express his ideal conceptions at all costs and the wish for an immediate reward in popular approval. He even loses his ability to retreat from the harsh world of fact into a satisfying world of dreams:

> if dreams were tried,
> His will swayed sicklily from side to side,
> Nor merely neutralised his waking act
> But tended e'en in fancy to distract
> The intermediate will, the choice of means.

He becomes incapable of any attempt to express himself: the 'intermediate will'—that faculty which mediates in all poets between the ideal conception and the expression in language— becomes stultified.

At this point in the action Browning informs us of the death of Adelaide, who, as the second wife of Ecelin Romano and guardian of Palma, his daughter by his first wife, had helped Salinguerra to keep Ecelin in the struggle for power in Italy. We hear the contents of the letter which Ecelin sends to Salinguerra, informing him of his decision to withdraw from political life and marry his three children to members of the Guelph party, so ending the strife. Browning tells us of Salinguerra's dash back from Naples and his arrival too late to prevent Ecelin from carrying out at least the first part of his intention. Salinguerra is left with Palma as a pawn in the political struggle. Sordello is chosen to sing the lay welcoming Salinguerra to the city of Mantua. Depressed and confused, he withdraws from

Mantua and wanders back to his old home at Goito, now deserted. There he retreats into his world of fancy:

> 'Twas Apollo now they lapped,
> Those mountains, not a pettish minstrel meant
> To wear his soul away in discontent,
> Brooding on fortune's malice.

There he remains and there we find him at the beginning of Book 3.

## Book 3

Sordello spends a year at Goito, forgetting Mantua and the failure of his ambitions, until a sudden inundation of the marsh below the castle brings him to think about his position in life again. He takes the inundation of the marsh by the sea as an example of the infinite capacity of Nature to retrieve her own mistakes. He realizes that his previous course of attempting to achieve the fulfilment of his spiritual nature in song was merely an instinctive striving towards his real aim. He now thinks that it is possible for him to achieve happiness, but only by different means. At this point occurs an important passage in which he makes a distinction between himself and ordinary people, based on his ability to identify himself with what he perceives outside himself. Ordinary people—

> with Being are endowed,
> However slight, distinct from what they See,
> However bounded. . . .

In this part of the poem, 'Being' is equivalent to the individual consciousness, and what people 'See' is equivalent to what is external to that individual consciousness. Sordello conceives his future course as the task of impressing his own individual nature on reality:

> To feed the first [Being] by gleanings from the last [the Seen],
> Attain its qualities, and slow or fast
> Become what they [other people] behold. . . .

Thus, he seeks to make an interpretation of reality in terms of his own existence.

There now occurs an important distinction which has already been referred to elsewhere in the poem—the distinction between body and soul. Sordello has already, by the power of his imagination, expressed himself in terms of his soul. He now seeks to express himself in terms of the body—materially:

> . . . [S]uch peace-in-strife,
> By transmutation, is the Use of Life,
> The Alien turning Native to the soul
> Or body—which instructs me; I am whole
> There [i.e. in the body] and demand a Palma; had the world
> Been from my soul to a like distance hurled,
> 'Twere Happiness to make it one with me. . . .

The basic meaning of this passage is that if Sordello's soul were as far from comprehending the external world as is his body from obtaining Palma as its mate, trying to comprehend it would make him happy. Why, then, should the gaining of Palma not also make him happy? Just as this understanding is reached, Naddo arrives to inform Sordello that Palma is betrothed to Count Richard Boniface but that the Count has been captured at the siege of Ferrara by Salinguerra. Palma sends a message by Naddo asking Sordello to come to her.

In one day and one night Sordello reaches Verona, and Browning begins again to describe the scene with which the poem began. While Sordello and Palma talk, the city of Verona arms to attack Ferrara and rescue Boniface. Palma tells Sordello that all her life she has felt the need for some one person with whom she can identify herself completely before she can achieve the fulfilment of her spiritual life. Sordello is that person. Palma tells him how she spent her childhood at Goito with the aged Adelaide, and how the latter, on her deathbed, had told Palma secrets which she had kept throughout her life. She also brings Sordello up to date with events that had occurred before and after his stay at Mantua. She now, as head of her house, bears her father's authority and asks Sordello to go with her to join Salinguerra and head the Ghibelline forces at Ferrara, representative, through her, of the authority of the Emperor. Sordello thus has an opportunity to act out his spiritual life and to make the people a manifestation of his will. They can be used as the extended body to his soul.

There now occurs another major shift in time and place. Leaving Palma and Sordello sleeping, Browning imagines himself at Venice, as he actually was in 1838. He addresses his readers directly and discusses the relative characteristics of the poetry of Eglamor and Sordello. He discusses the songs of the two poets in order to express the fact that Sordello's song bears the same relation to his spiritual life as the sailor's stay on land during a calm at sea bears to his. The song of Eglamor was really perfect, but limited; Sordello's was more all-embracing, but never fully realized. Then the poet speaks of himself as looking over the Venetian scene for an individual who could be taken as representative of human life. He selects, not the fresh maidens of the town and the country, but a jaded beggar. He says that the point which he wishes to make by this selection is one which has been important in his own development:

> I ask youth and strength
> And health for each of you, not more—at length
> Grown wise, who asked *at home* that the whole race
> Might add the spirit's to the body's grace,
> And all be dizened out as chiefs and bards.          (my italics)

This passage suggests that it was during his visit to Italy in 1838 that he first underwent a modification of his earlier idealism. Venice, he says, has taught him the value of mere life, and led him to realize that living involves an inevitable admixture of good and evil. Browning addresses the beggar (who is also a prostitute) as if she were his mistress. He takes her as typical of unhappy humanity, suggesting to him that even in evil there is some awareness of good. He insists on the importance of this perception:

> A slight advance,—
> Merely to find the sickness you die through,
> And nought beside! but if one can't eschew
> One's portion in the common lot, at least
> One can avoid an ignorance increased
> Tenfold by dealing out hint after hint
> How nought were like dispensing without stint
> The water of life—

This last alternative of over-idealism is what he has already confessed to being guilty of. Now he says that human life is spent in creating a complex engine by means of which Man is to act. But life is too short for its completion, and each death leaves the process to be begun again. Humanity, in the past, the present and the future, has a limited capacity—even the best can only extend to others their own limited perception:

> The office of ourselves . . .
>                           has been,
> For the worst of us, to say they so have seen;
> For the better, what it was they saw; for the best
> Impart the gift of seeing to the rest. . . .

At this point Browning digresses to a justification of his own perception and his own method of representing it. He conjectures that at some time in the future, Seeing, which is the function of the poet, and Doing, which is that of the man of action, will be united in one man. Meanwhile, when it is only possible for the individual to do one or the other, Browning will play the part of the poet. Let those who think that they can make better men than Sordello, he says, beware lest they meet the fate of those who would have sacrificed Hercules to the Egyptian god. With a reference to the poet Landor, and to Miss Haworth, one of Browning's oldest friends, he ends the digression and returns to the matter of his poem—the fate of the noble soul who ignores the limitations of his own human life, and, in doing so, falls short of the greatness which there was in him to achieve. The Book closes with the story of St. John's mis-

44

taking his own portrait for the devil—a warning to the reader as to how he should read the poem. The reader should not take Sordello's portrait as St. John took his own, but should look closely in order to detect in the hero of the poem traits of his own character.

## Book 4

When we last heard of Sordello he was in Verona. The fourth Book opens in Ferrara, whither he has travelled with Palma. There is first a vivid description of the misery caused by the war to both those of the Guelph and the Ghibelline factions. From the city we move to Salinguerra's palace, where Count Richard Boniface is imprisoned. Here we see Sordello again. He reviews his determination to use the people as an expression of his will—as the body to his soul—and now realizes for the first time that this involves making them happy. Only Salinguerra can help him towards his aim, and it is to him that Sordello goes.

The result of his first, hour-long interview with the warrior is despair. Sordello, prematurely aged, weak and ineffective, is incapable of bringing the youthful, powerful man of action to the service of his idea. Sordello wanders out into the war-stricken city, understanding for the first time the degradation which war brings to the people. Palma finds him singing to a group of soldiers who have recognized his minstrel's garb. She takes him back to Salinguerra and it is in the scene which follows that we come face to face with the warrior for the first time. The two men are each other's opposites, and to Salinguerra, who has in his age kept the freshness of youth, the poet, physically weakened by a life of self-indulgent imaginings, is something to be used—if only a use can be found. As Salinguerra searches for some method of employing Sordello, he reviews his own youth and the events which have led up to the present.

Meanwhile Sordello and Palma discuss the question which Sordello's wanderings through the city have brought into his mind. It has occurred to him that if men, before they can be used for his purpose, must be made happy, then the cause which he follows must be the one which is most likely to bring them happiness. Which is the right cause, Guelph or Ghibelline? Or, on the other hand—

> What if there remained
> A cause intact, distinct from these, ordained
> For me, its true discoverer?

This undiscovered cause has already been suggested to Sordello by the soldier who asked him for a song. This cause is that of Rome—the ideal of ancient Rome, which is to be the means of the unification of Italy!

## Book 5

Another day in the war-stricken city is enough to shatter this dream of the ennoblement of men in the service of the new cause. Sordello realizes that this may still come in the future, but all the use it is to him in the present is in giving him the credit of first conceiving it. At this point Sordello makes a further realization: for the first time he thinks—

> God has conceded two sights to a man—
> One, of men's whole work, time's completed plan,
> The other, of the minute's work, man's first
> Step to the plan's completedness: what's dispersed
> Save hope of that supreme step . . .?

He now understands that while the vision of the unification of Italy is the ultimate end, a work which can only be completed in the future, there yet remains to him the task of taking the first immediate step to the distant goal. At the same time he makes a perception which is an essential part of Browning's idea of life: that—

> . . . Collective man
> Outstrips the individual.

The great design cannot be achieved at once, in the Now, but only in the Then. In the future will come the perfection of the

46

union between Strength (as shown in physical action) and Knowledge (as shown in the all-embracing action of the soul). In the meantime his task is to make a present and imperfect combination of Strength and Knowledge in the cause of mankind. Salinguerra must be persuaded to espouse the Guelph cause and take the first step towards freeing the Italian people from the political domination of the Emperor.

His first attempt to do this fails. In his effort to persuade Salinguerra, Sordello is too conscious of himself and pleads without earnestness. Consequently Salinguerra is unmoved:

> Then a flash of bitter truth:
> So fantasies could break and fritter youth
> That he had long ago lost earnestness,
> Lost will to work, lost power to even express
> The need of working!

Yet the contempt of Salinguerra, even though smilingly expressed, spurs Sordello to a new effort of persuasion and gives him the earnestness he needs. In this new attempt, the accumulated perceptions of his life burst forth. The Knowledge which he has to utter is beyond his age, but he pleads for it with complete conviction and absorption in the truth of his argument. Sordello pleads his own failure as an argument for Salinguerra's success. He demonstrates his conception of the continuous development of the human race. He now realizes that the function that he should have fulfilled was the visioning of the Truth which could be acted on in the immediate present. In ignoring the limitations of human life and fixing his gaze on the wider Truth, he has missed his opportunity and wasted his life and power. But he urges Salinguerra to take up the task—to work out the plan of God and be the first to espouse the cause of humanity.

Salinguerra is not convinced, but he is moved enough by Sordello's earnestness and the force of his personality to throw, half in fancy, the imperial baldric round the neck of the younger man. At this, all three stand silent, affected by some truth which they can barely perceive. It is only now that Palma reveals the secret that she learned from her father in the monastery—that Sordello is Salinguerra's son. Salinguerra is overcome. Half-raving in his hope of future success, he lays plans for the action which must follow in the future. Sordello stands silent. He is now faced with the great temptation. From his father he can receive the power of the Empire, and, married to Palma, can be the lord of Italy. Palma, seeing his hesitant state of mind, draws Salinguerra away, and they wait in a room below until they hear the stamp of Sordello's foot upon the floor.

*Book 6*

This final Book contains the thoughts of Sordello as he struggles with the temptation and wins a new nobility in the struggle. Left alone to consider what he should do, he takes the moon which shines through the window as the symbol of his ideal, as the individual concept of Truth which until now he had lacked:

> So had Sordello been, by consequence,
> Without a function: others made pretence
> To strength not half his own, yet had some core
> Within, submitted to some moon, before
> Them still, superior still whate'er their force,—
> Were able therefore to fulfil a course. . . .

Sordello now has the ideal which he has always lacked—the service of the people and the eventual unification of his country. He perceives that this is a higher ideal than that which suffices for others—it is higher than the love which impels Palma and the hate which drives Salinguerra on against his enemies. The question now becomes one of whether he can remain true to his ideal in the face of great temptation.

He is tempted to temporize with what he knows to be the Truth and to identify the good of the people with his own advantage. He sees through the first argument which his worse nature puts forward. He knows that, although the world has never yet achieved the whole, or even an appreciable part, of the Truth, yet it has always been in the world:

48

> . . . 'tis like at no one time
> Of the world's story has not truth, the prime
> Of truth, the very truth which, loosed, had hurled
> The world's course right, been really in the world. . . .

He knows that he should remain true to the gleam of Truth which he has caught. His lower nature prompts him to ask himself whether it is right that he should sacrifice himself to his ideal. The decision would be easy were the issue a simple one of right or wrong, but both Guelph and Ghibelline factions are human in their mixture of good and evil. He has to answer the question of whether an improvement of the condition of the people would really benefit them. In the present state of human life, the people seek the whole of Truth by seeking small parts of it:

> The Whole they seek by Parts—but, found that Whole,
> Could they revert, enjoy past gains?

If there is no certainty of his self-sacrifice bringing permanent good, there *is* certainty that he could obtain his own good out of their misery. The enjoyment of his own life in the present would not substantially affect the achievement of their betterment in the future:

> Speed their Then, but how
> This badge would suffer you improve your Now!
>
> Oh, 'twere too absurd to slight
> For the hereafter the today's delight!

This is the temptation which, in a different context, also assailed Paracelsus. He succumbed to it and lost sight of the ideal of service which had led him to devote himself to the service of the people. Sordello escapes the trap which caught Paracelsus.

Sordello's escape is made possible by the certainty which his new sense of purpose gives him. He knows what course of action he should follow because he is conscious of his failure in the past. At this point Browning breaks into the meditations of his hero in order to summarize the significance of the stage of spiritual development which Sordello had reached. All his life, Browning comments, he had been wrong, but he reached and held the Truth at the last:

> . . . the sudden swell
> Of his expanding soul showed Ill and Well,
> Sorrow and Joy, Beauty and Ugliness,
> Virtue and Vice, the Larger and the Less,
> All qualities, in fine, recorded here,
> Might be but modes of Time and this one sphere,
> Urgent on these, but not of force to bind
> Eternity. . . .

The essential meaning of this passage is that the disparity between good and evil which every thinking man sees in life is not a part of the Truth, but merely a condition of the imperfection of the temporal world. In Eternity, good will emerge in its purity. Browning continues to investigate the relationship between Time and Eternity, expanding this passage into a statement of his most basic ideas.

Browning says that the relationship between Time and Eternity is that the former is contained within the latter. A similar relationship exists between Matter and Mind. Smallness and greatness, sorrow and joy, are things which have no meaning in Eternity. The task of the visionary is the perception of the reality of Eternity and the eternal pattern behind the sham reality of life circumscribed by Time—life which begins with birth and ends with death. The task of each individual is to exercise Mind on Matter—to make the body which dies the medium of expression for the soul which does not die. This is what Sordello has failed to do. As Browning pointed out in Book 2, Sordello tried to express his soul in terms of itself; he tried to express the visions which his imagination had given to him in their pure form. What he should have done was to seek for a temporal, or physical, expression of his visions, which would have resulted in concrete benefit to himself and to other men. It is only at the end of his life that he fully understands this. To him, as to Paracelsus, Truth comes in life, but only just before death. The strain of the spiritual struggle is too much for his weakened frame. When Palma and Salinguerra enter they find him dead; the baldric, symbol of imperial power, which his father had thrown round his neck, lies beneath his foot.

Such an account of the poem as the above makes obvious the truth of Elizabeth Barrett's criticism of the poem. *Sordello* has a very inadequate structure. There is no clear principle governing the sequence of events. The frequent changes in time and place combine with the complexity of the background material of the story to make it almost incomprehensible to the ordinary reader. The reason for this incoherency is probably to be found in the way in which the poem was written. Browning changed his mind about the composition of the poem four times during a period of seven years (see DeVane's Handbook) and this process left its mark on the structure.

THE VERSE OF SORDELLO

The verse of *Sordello* is no clearer than the narrative structure. The heroic couplet tends to feature the firm, end-stopped line with the positive break or caesura in the middle of the line. Consequently it is not the best kind of verse to choose for a long narrative and discursive poem. This is not to say that the form cannot be used for these purposes—both Dryden and Pope handle it with great effect in both narrative and discourse. But Browning lacked, at this stage in his career, the technical proficiency needed before the form can be used in this way. All too frequently the constriction of the couplet form forced him into the obscurity which we see in the lines:

> Soul on Matter being thrust,
> Joy comes when so much Soul is wreaked in Time
> On Matter: let the Soul's attempt sublime
> Matter beyond the scheme and so prevent
> By more or less that deed's accomplishment,
> And Sorrow follows. . . .
>
> SORDELLO 6

51

In line three of this passage the word 'Matter' is used as a noun. In line four it may be used either as a noun or as a verb, making two possible readings. If the word is read as a verb the line reads:

> If the sublime attempt of the Soul matters more than the scheme. . . .

If it is read as a noun:

> Let the attempt of the Soul make Matter sublime. . . .

Ambiguity can be a source of strength in poetry, but here it is simply harmful, interfering with our reception of Browning's argument and making it impossible to decide on the reading which he wishes us to take. The context of the passage makes the first reading appear the right one—it describes the fault of Sordello himself, who is wrong not in attempting to sublimate Matter, but in thinking primarily of the means rather than the end, and of the fame which he can obtain for himself. A tendency towards this kind of writing is present in all Browning's early verse—but nowhere is it as pronounced as in the heroic couplets of *Sordello*.

In this respect the blank verse of *Paracelsus* is more satisfactory. However, the verse of that poem is marred by the feature which is also shared by that of *Pauline* and *Sordello*. In all these poems there is a tendency towards an excessive use of metaphor and simile. Thus, in Book 1 of *Sordello*, when Browning wishes to indicate the way in which support for the Guelph cause has grown in Italy, shrouding the early success of the Ghibelline, he enters into a twenty-two line metaphor concerning cliffs, raised by an earthquake and made to abut into the sea, gradually being choked in sea-weed. The metaphor almost becomes an allegory. It is so long and complex that the reader finds it a major difficulty firstly to follow the development of the metaphor, and secondly to relate it to the political situation. In *Pauline*, the same characteristic is shown at an early stage; and in this poem neither simile nor metaphor is involved with the argument; rather, they are used as ornament, with no organic connection with the train of thought.

Browning wrote to Elizabeth Barrett in February 1846:

> Of course an artist's whole problem must be, as Carlyle wrote to me, 'the expressing with articulate clearness the thought in him'—I am almost inclined to say that *clear expression* should be his only work and care—for he is born, ordained, such as he is—and not born learned in putting what was born in him into words—what ever *can* be clearly spoken, ought to be. But 'bricks and mortar' is very easily said. . . .

*Sordello* would have been a far better poem had Browning followed his own dictum. For *Sordello* he chose the wrong type of brick, and he took no care to ensure that the poem was built according to an adequate design. The result was that his career received a serious set-back, from which it took some time to recover. Yet *Sordello* was the last of the poems written in the early manner. Its composition obviously allowed Browning to work out certain ideas which were very important to him, and to formulate fully the body of doctrine which remained unchanged throughout his life. In that *Sordello* gave him the opportunity to do this, and so set his mind at rest for the time being and allowed him to concentrate on the form of his poetry, it cannot be regretted. Five years after its publication he was in the process of working out the form which was to enable him to achieve his greatest work. Meanwhile, since 1837, he had been writing plays. In his attempts to achieve success on the stage we see him writing his way towards the form most suitable to his talent—the form of the dramatic monologue. In the meantime, however, he was enthusiastically setting out to embody, in purely dramatic and objective form, the ideas which the early poems had given him the scope to develop.

## 2

# An Attempt at the Stage

It was after the dinner at which the young author of *Paracelsus* received the compliments of Wordsworth that Charles Macready is supposed to have asked Browning to write him a play, and stop him from going to America. The dinner took place on 26 March, 1836. Later that month Browning wrote to Macready:

> I am now engaged in a work which is nearly done: I allow myself a month to complete it: from the first of July I shall be free: if, before then, any subject shall suggest itself to you— I will give you my whole heart and soul to the writing of a Tragedy on it to be ready by the first of November next. . . .

The subject which was eventually chosen grew out of Browning's work on the biography of Wentworth, Earl of Strafford. John Forster, who had written a complimentary review of *Paracelsus* for *The Examiner,* had been commissioned to write a biography of Strafford. Browning had met him at Macready's home and the two men had become friends. Then, when Forster fell ill before he had completed the book, Browning stepped in and helped him to finish it. This was in February and March of 1836. As a result, when he decided to take the subject of Strafford for his tragedy, he already had the materials to hand.

Once the play was written Macready began to have doubts as to its suitability for stage performance. He wrote in his diary on 19 March 1837:

Read *Strafford* in the evening, which I fear is too historical; it is the policy of the man and its consequence upon him, not the heart, temper, feelings, that work on this policy . . .

What Macready noticed, Browning acknowledged in the preface to the first edition of the play:

> I had for some time been engaged in a Poem of a very different nature, when induced to make the present attempt; and am not without apprehension that my eagerness to freshen a jaded mind by diverting it to the healthy natures of a grand epoch, may have operated unfavourably on the represented play, which is *one of Action in Character, rather than Character in Action.* . . .
>
> (my italics)

This is more or less what he had said in the preface to *Paracelsus* (quoted on p. 21).

These statements amount to a declaration that the poet is not focusing his attention on the behaviour of his characters and so revealing their nature, but is concerned to direct attention primarily to the character itself. That the two statements are so similar is significant. *Paracelsus* was not meant for performance; but *Strafford* was! The stage play does have a greater degree of economy and tension than the dramatic poem, but it has always been regarded as having been a comparative failure. The reason for this is not that it contains too much psychological and philosophical matter, but that Browning took insufficient care to make real the connection between this material and the actual behaviour of his characters.

Browning's main aim in *Strafford* was the delineation of a man of undoubted and unshakable nobility, torn between two ideas—love for his country and love for his king. In order that this object should be successfully achieved it was necessary not only that we should see the symptoms of the dilemma in Strafford himself, but that both alternatives should be put before us in such a way as to make us understand why he should feel any dilemma at all. The blank verse in which the play is written does not help towards this end. The bareness and simplicity of the verse indicates the extent to which Browning was trying to adapt his art to the purpose in hand, but it is too stilted to achieve any impression of real dialogue. Nor is it helpful to the reader of the play that Browning assumes a thorough familiarity with the events on which its action is based.

However, the major fault of the play is caused by Browning's failure to make the motivation of the central character real to his audience. Strafford himself is rendered with considerable vitality. His love for his country is established indirectly by means of his friendship with Pym, which we hear about in the first scene. The scene with his children at the end of the play, and his relationship with Lady Carlisle, also help to make him real and to arouse the interest of the audience in his character and the reasons for his actions. However, the presentation of Strafford turns on one main point—his love for the king. The latter is presented as weak, vacillating, mistrustful and foolish. It is part of Browning's conception that he should be all these things and that he should not *deserve* the love of Strafford. Yet if there is no reason in the character of Charles why he should be loved, that is all the more reason why the character of Strafford should provide an explanation. The love is unreasonable and yet we are given no understanding of why Strafford has it. Consequently, everything which depends on that love as a motivating force fails to become real.

### 'KING VICTOR AND KING CHARLES'

Browning's next play is not a great improvement in this respect. *King Victor and King Charles* was published on 12 March 1842 as the second volume in the series of poems and plays which Browning called *Bells and Pomegranates*. The focal point is again the soul of the hero. As the title suggests, the play is based on the tension between King Victor of Sardinia and his son, King Charles. We are primarily interested in the development of the soul of King Charles from apparent weakness to strength and determination. King Victor is the type of ruler who subdues all interests to that of the throne, which his own efforts have created. With Charles stands Polyxena, his wife, who is motivated chiefly by her love for her husband. Between Charles and his father shifts the political minister D'Ormea, unscrupulous and time-serving.

The play is divided into four parts, each part manifesting a particular aspect of the character of either Victor or Charles.

## 'King Victor' Part 1

At the beginning of the play we learn from a conversation between Charles and Polyxena that Charles has obeyed the command of his father to present himself before the assembled court. He does not know the reason for the command but suspects that it is his father's intention to deprive him of the succession to the throne in favour of an illegitimate son. Charles had spent his youth under the domination of his father and his elder brother, who is now dead. Victor had never tried to conceal the contempt which he felt for the character of Charles. A conversation which Charles has with D'Ormea, whom he despises as a time-server, leaves him with the idea that his suspicion was correct. Yet Charles determines to obey his father whatever he demands, and he and Polyxena look forward to a life of quiet happiness together.

## 'King Victor' Part 2

In this part we discover from the conversation between Victor and D'Ormea, that the real intention of Victor is not to prevent Charles from succeeding, but actually to abdicate in his favour. As a result of his ambitious and unscrupulous policies the state of the country is serious. At home, the people are dissatisfied; abroad, Spain and Austria are combined in disgust at his dishonesty. Victor plans to abdicate in Charles's favour in order that the monarchy shall be preserved from danger. Because Charles was known to be ignorant of his father's dishonesty and severity, he would be able to make peace with the foreign powers and placate the people.

D'Ormea urges Victor against this idea, mainly through self-interest. He is afraid that his own life will be the price of a bargain with Spain and Austria. He warns Victor that he is too much of a king to be able to retire to a life of inaction, and that his abdication will be a source of constant regret to him. Charles, shocked at the idea of taking his father's place, pleads with him to relinquish the plan. When his father insists, he obeys him and assumes the crown, ignorant of the real motive behind Victor's action. Polyxena suspects some ulterior purpose, but is unable to see what it is. She also urges Victor with pleading and taunts to re-assume the throne. The scene ends with the suggestion of alienation between Charles and Polyxena because he will accept no suspicion of his father.

### 'King Charles' Part 1

This scene opens one year after the abdication, with D'Ormea attempting to persuade Polyxena that Victor intends to return and seize the throne while Charles is away concluding terms of peace with Spain and Austria. In the year which has passed since Victor's abdication Charles has, by wisdom and kindness, restored the kingdom to a state of health. Charles returns just as Polyxena is finally won over to D'Ormea's opinion of Victor. Charles rejects D'Ormea's accusations and dismisses them both. He then leaves the stage himself. Now Victor enters, and his soliloquy proves that D'Ormea's accusations were correct. He has returned in order to seize power from his son. He is aware of the falseness and deceit which is involved, but is determined to carry out his intention in spite of his own shame. When Charles returns he is in the process of tearing the papers which contain the evidence against his father. Seeing Victor before him, he refuses to acknowledge the real motive for his father's sudden return and when D'Ormea and Polyxena re-enter and state their suspicions, Charles protects Victor by pretending a false motive for his appearance.

### 'King Charles' Part 2

The final scene begins with a soliloquy by D'Ormea, from which we gather that he has determined to be honest in his future dealings with the two kings. When Charles and Polyxena enter he tells them that Victor has been plotting again and attempting to bribe leading men in the state to support him against his son. In reply Charles gives D'Ormea full powers of arrest against all the people whom he suspects of being implicated with Victor. This is not an indication of trust in D'Ormea, but a challenge to his minister to prove his allegations:

> The whole thing is a lie, a hateful lie,
> As I believed and as my father said.
> I knew it from the first, but was compelled
> To circumvent you. . . .

Yet it is only when D'Ormea has gone on his errand that we learn that Charles knew that the allegations were true, but that he had made up his mind to obey his father again and return the crown to him. Polyxena urges him to keep the crown in spite of the unhappiness which it will give him, in order that he should be able to go on serving the people.

When Victor enters and demands the crown Charles gives it to him because he recognizes a higher duty even than that of serving the people. Victor takes the crown and with it he assumes the knowledge of his coming death. Before he dies, however, he learns for the first time the truly noble nature of his son, and sees the possibilities of honest rule:

> . . . I seem learning many other things
> Because the time for using them is past.
> If 'twere to do again! That's idly wished.
> Truthfulness might prove policy as good
> As guile.

His last act is the defiance of D'Ormea:

> You lied, D'Ormea! I do not repent.

This last statement contradicts the apparent conclusion which his action has led us to. It indicates that at the last moment, if not before, he was capable of conceiving of the self-sacrifice in the cause of a noble sentiment which was shown in the behaviour of his son.

As this outline of the play shows, it does not contain much action. Yet this alone would not be sufficient reason for Macready's refusal to perform it, or for the general decision of the critics that it is a relative failure. The verse of the play is better adapted to dialogue than is that of *Strafford* and it is better constructed. The main fault of the play lies in the fact that, as in *Strafford*, we are not given sufficient evidence of the mental struggles which form the real action. Browning is not interested in external action, but nor is he really interested in internal action. The play is a *demonstration* of nobility of character. Charles is governed throughout by a nobility of sentiment which makes him subjugate all his more or less selfish desires to the principle of obedience. He refuses to recognize the deceit which his father is practising. At the end, Victor, too, becomes capable of real nobility of spirit. Even D'Ormea turns honest. Yet Browning does not present his characters as people so much as types of a certain spiritual cast. We do not see or feel the reasons which make them act as they do. Thus, all that we learn about the change of mind which is central to the presentation of D'Ormea is in his one speech:

> D'Ormea was wicked, say, some twenty years;
> A tree so long was stunted; afterward,
> What if it grew, continued growing, till
> No fellow of the forest equalled it?

All this speech contains is a statement that he has changed his mind and decided to be honest in future. There is nothing in the verse to make us really believe in the change of mind—no indication of any psychological development. This is so throughout the play. We have to deduce the motivation from dialogue and soliloquy and presume that the characters on the stage are going through some kind of mental struggle. Nothing is brought home to us with any dramatic power.

'THE RETURN OF THE DRUSES'
Like *King Victor and King Charles*, Browning's third play met with the disapproval of Macready. By this time Macready was

becoming seriously disturbed about Browning's ability to write successfully. He wrote in his diary:

> Read Browning's play and with the deepest concern, I yield to the belief that he will *never write again*—to any purpose. I fear his intellect is not quite clear. I do not know how to write to Browning.

It is not difficult to understand the reason for his despair. The two previous plays, with all their faults, had been attempts on the part of the author to achieve the discipline of his powers necessary before he could write successfully for the stage. *The Return of the Druses,* published in January 1843, as number four of *Bells and Pomegranates,* is in part a return to the manner of the earlier poetry. The subject of the play is more exotic than that of either of the others. The setting is—

> An Islet of the Southern Sporades, colonized by the Druses of Lebanon and garrisoned by the Knights-Hospitallers of Rhodes.

The matter of the play is the history of the Druses, who, many years before the point at which the play begins, had been driven from Lebanon by Turkish forces. Their leaders had called for assistance to the Knights-Hospitallers, but had been slain by them and their people placed under the tyrannical authority of a Prefect. The main character of the play is Djabal, the only surviving member of the ruling Druse families. Djabal spent his youth wandering through Europe, acquiring a certain amount of European knowledge, by means of which he has imposed on the naive Druses, so that they think him the re-incarnation of their dead leader and god, Hakeem.

The play begins with Djabal having arranged that the initiated Druses slay the Prefect on his return from Rhodes. Once that is done the people will embark in the galleys of Venice for Lebanon. The island is to be ceded to the Venetians in exchange for conveyance to the Lebanon. The Druses believe that once the killing has been effected Djabal will undergo a transformation and become Hakeem before them, with divine powers.

Among the most fervent of Djabal's supporters are Khalil and his sister, Anael, who is selected as the bride of Djabal. What none of the Druses know is that Loys de Dreux, son of the Duke of Bretagne and friend of Djabal, has taken the cause of the Druses to heart and pleaded it with such effect at Rhodes, that the Prefect has been deprived of his office and his power transferred to Loys and the Papal Legate. Loys himself, however, is unaware of the fact that the Prefect, fearing assassination, has bribed the Chapter of the Order to allow him to retire.

What interests Browning in this situation is the issue which it involves between truth and falsehood, particularly in their relationship to love. As the play opens, we see that Djabal is tormented with doubts as to whether he was justified in saving his people by deceit. At the root of his concern is his love for Anael. He cannot bear to think that her love for him is based on the lie that he is Hakeem. Anael herself is a study in purity and nobility of soul. At the beginning of the play she is troubled because she does not think herself worthy to become the bride of Hakeem. As a result she plans to take the murder of the Prefect on herself in order to expiate her human weakness. When she learns from Djabal that he is not Hakeem, she has just committed the murder. She leaves Djabal and goes to betray him to the guards of the Nuncio. As Djabal is seized by the guards Loys enters. He refuses to believe the charges which are made against his friend. Djabal replies to them by saying that if a Druse has betrayed him—thus making his deception pointless—then he will commit suicide. The scene which follows shows the uninitiated Druses being worked on by the Nuncio to turn on Djabal. Anael is brought in, veiled. Her brother Khalil tears the veil from her and in the scene which follows Loys and Djabal plead with her for her love. Loys, now disillusioned as to the nature of the Order which he would have joined, and so free of his vow of celibacy, accuses Djabal of being unworthy of Anael's love:

Who's worth her, I or thou? I—who for Anael
Uprightly, purely kept my way, the long

True way—left thee each by-path, boldly lived
Without the lies and blood,—or thou, or thou?

Act 5

In reply, Djabal makes no claim to be worthy. He sees his true
greatness as lost in the fatal division between the wisdom he
learned in Europe and the instinct he retained with his race.
Now nothing is left him of his false nature, but—

> . . . from out their crash,
> A third and better nature rises up—
> My mere man's-nature!

Act 5

Witnessing the nobility of his new humbleness, Anael realizes
fully for the first time, the true human greatness of the man that
she loves, and she dies with the recognition of it on her lips—

Hakeem!

The Druses take her death as the effect of Djabal's divinity
and seize on the Nuncio and his guards. Djabal inspires the
people with their belief, and, having assured himself of the
safety of the enterprise and delegated his authority to Khalil, he
stabs himself. As he does so, the Venetians who are to carry the
Druses back to Lebanon, enter. Supported by Khalil and Loys,
Djabal takes a few steps towards the shore, cries out a final
encouragement to the Druses, and dies.

The love relationship of Anael and Djabal is the central part
of the play. Writing to his friend, Miss Haworth, some years
before the play was published, Browning had said:

> I want a subject of the most wild and passionate love, to contrast
> with the one I mean to have ready in a short time (probably
> *King Victor and King Charles*). I have many half-conceptions,
> floating fancies: give me your notion of a thorough self-
> devotement, self-forgetting; should it be a woman who loves
> thus, or a man?

He embodied this conception in the character of Anael. But in the characters of Loys and Djabal he embodied the conceptions of conduct which had been developing since the time when he was re-moulding *Sordello*. Both characters are formed on a concept of duty to humanity. Both are complicated by the fact that they contain an association between the love of humanity and the love of one individual.

The play is considerably more complex than either of those which preceded it and it also contains more dramatic power. The verse is more ornate in order to convey some suggestion of the exoticism of the subject. Some of the scenes are very successful. When the Prefect declares his relief at his replacement by Loys, and his consequent escape from death, he stands at the entrance to an alcove. We know that within the alcove Anael is waiting to kill him. The result is a strong sense of dramatic irony. When Anael falls dead in the pressure of her emotion, Khalil thinks that Djabal has killed her because she doubted him. His faith in Djabal is pathetic as he pleads that he bring her back to life.

The whole play is, in fact, more dramatic than *Strafford* or *King Victor and King Charles*. The complexity and partial obscurity of the action tend to make it unsuitable for production, but it contains an organic relationship between action and character. For the first time Browning has succeeded in making motivation real. The play would be better if there were a more simple and evident relationship between the real subject matter (love), and the apparent subject matter (the history of the Druses). In his next play Browning attempted to combine both simplicity and dramatic power.

'A BLOT ON THE SCUTCHEON'
*A Blot on the Scutcheon* was written some time towards the end of 1840 and published on the day of its first performance, in February 1843. It was Browning's last attempt to write a play for Macready to produce, and the quarrel which developed during its preparation for the stage created a degree of bad feeling between Browning and both Macready and Forster,

and put an end to his friendship with both of them for a number of years. Macready was again doubtful about the quality of the play, but his doubts were partially allayed by the extremely favourable opinion of Charles Dickens, who had been given the play to read. According to Dickens *A Blot on the Scutcheon* was—

> ... a tragedy that *must* be played: and must be played, moreover by Macready.

Consequently Macready went ahead with the production although in so half-hearted a manner that Browning became seriously annoyed. Eventually the play was acted on 11 February, and was published on the same day. Browning had asked his publisher, Moxon, to rush it through the press in order to prevent Macready from making any serious alterations in the text for performance.

Browning went to considerable lengths to date the action of his play, but it gives to the modern reader an unmistakable flavour of nineteenth-century England. The manners of the characters and their setting may belong to the eighteenth century, but the ideas which move them are certainly those of the age of Queen Victoria. The story is not complex. The younger sister of Thorold, Earl Tresham, is in love with Henry, Earl of Merton. They had met by chance in the country, and the relationship had grown almost in spite of them. He had grown into the habit of visiting Mildred in her chamber at night with the natural result that they anticipated marriage and brought a 'blot' to the family scutcheon. They plan to recover the position by marriage. Consequently, Henry pays a formal visit to Mildred's brother and asks for her hand in marriage (both her parents being dead). Tresham asks his sister if she is willing to marry Henry and receives an affirmative answer. It is at this point that Tresham is approached by Gerard, an old family servant. Gerard has for some time been aware of the fact that Mildred is being visited at night, although he does not know the identity of her lover. Torn between his affection for Mildred and his sense of the honour of the family which he serves, he eventually tells Tresham what has been going on.

Tresham accuses his sister and she confesses her guilt by silence. What infuriates him is that she still persists in her desire to marry Henry and will not reveal the name of her seducer so that she can be married to him instead. Tresham is disgusted at what seems to be the implication, denounces her to his brother Austin and his fiancée Guendolen, and rushes out. Mildred faints with the shock of her brother's denunciation of her. Guendolen asserts her faith in the essential innocence of Mildred and a few moments alone with her are enough to enable her to unravel the secret—that the lover and Henry are one and the same. Meanwhile, Tresham has hurried away into the woods, and does not return until midnight, when Henry, in ignorance of what has happened, has come to visit Mildred for the last time before their marriage. Tresham, unaware of his identity, accosts him and forces him to reveal himself and fight. Henry does not defend himself, and falls. He dies, after having sent a message of love to Mildred. Austin and Guendolen rush in—too late. Tresham goes to break the news to Mildred. She forgives him and dies of excess of grief with her arms round his neck. Austin and Guendolen again arrive too late. They are in time to hear Tresham's last speech, admitting that he was wrong—

Vengeance is God's, not man's. Remember me!

He has taken poison.

In simplicity of outline and clearness of structure the play is a definite improvement on those which preceded it. The indirectness of the opening scene is clever. We learn about the coming of Henry by hearing the conversation of the servants who are watching it, and at the same time are made aware of the attitude of Gerard. Thus, from the beginning of the play, we are aware that there exists the possibility of a tragic conclusion. The scene also suggests the disparity between appearance and reality which is central to the action of the play. What Browning is concerned to demonstrate in the play is not as simple as might at first sight appear. He is saying that the behaviour of the lovers is wrong in so far as they attempt to base their happiness on untruth, but also that Tresham is wrong in his violent reaction. Tresham's passionate disgust at the apparent perfidy of the sister whom he had hitherto regarded as perfectly pure and chaste, leads him to accept a false appearance. The resultant delusion is productive of more misery and destruction than the first. It is the accumulation of failure to keep to truth or reality which brings about the tragic conclusion.

Dickens found the play intensely moving. For him Mildred's recurrent complaint that she was motherless in extenuation of her 'fall' was deeply pathetic. It is doubtful if any modern reader could feel quite what Dickens felt, but the reason for this lies within the play rather than in any change of ideas during the intervening period. For a drama to be successful in *any* age, the motivation of the characters must be based on characteristics which people of all ages have in common. The concept of female purity was important to Browning and Dickens in a way in which it is not important to us, but this is not what matters. What *does* matter is that we should understand why this concept should have such a strong influence on the minds of the characters and have led them to act in the way they did. Browning makes no attempt to do this. The power of the concept is *assumed* rather than demonstrated. As a result, we— who tend to reject the concept of purity as a motivating factor of sufficient importance to produce tragedy in our own day— are unconvinced by the violence with which Tresham acts. Browning prepared to make this demonstration by introducing Guendolen and Austin, two characte, who do not feel as strongly about Mildred's purity as they do about ordinary human love, but he does not complete it. He does not seem to be interested in psychological development so much as in certain abstract concepts and their influence on certain states of mind. Thus, in spite of the lively element of what Browning called 'drabbing and stabbing', the play fails to be convincing to the modern reader. Macready reported that when the play was read to the actors in his company, they laughed. We tend to react in much the same way.

Because he had quarrelled with Macready over the production of *A Blot on the Scutcheon,* Browning submitted his next play to the rival producer Charles Keane. This play was *Colombe's Birthday,* which Keane agreed to produce on the condition that Browning waited for nearly two years, without publishing it first. Browning wrote to his friend, Christopher Dowson, telling him of the proposal and saying,

> I . . . *will* do no such thing as let this new work lie stifled for a year and odd,—and work double-tides to bring out something as likely to be popular this present season—for something I *must* print, or risk the hold, such as it is, I have at present on *my* public. . . .

The play was published in the following month, April 1844.

The plot is quite simple. Colombe, Duchess of Cleves and Juliers, holds the Duchy on false grounds. The true claimant, Prince Berthold, is approaching her court to present his claims and displace her. Among all the crowd of officials and courtiers no one can be found whose concern for Colombe is greater than his concern for himself, to carry the news to her. The courtiers trick Valence, a poor advocate from Cleves, who has come to plead the cause of his famine-stricken city, into delivering the news. When he learns the truth of the situation he is the only person who stands by Colombe, while the courtiers plan the transfer of their allegiance to the new Duke.

Berthold arrives in advance of his bodyguard, accompanied only by his scholarly companion, Melchior. He is met by Valence with Colombe's defiance and retires, saying that he will return that night when Colombe has had time to consider the evidence which he presents as to the legality of his claim. Colombe delegates to Valence the responsibility of deciding on the claim. This places him in a difficult position, for he, meanwhile, has

68

guessed that there is a chance that she will return the love which he has conceived for her, and realizes that if he decides that she has the right to the Duchy then he will be deprived of the chance of marrying her. As he reaches a decision and is on his way to tell her that Berthold is the rightful claimant, he meets Berthold, who has returned before the appointed time because he has decided to offer marriage to Colombe. Valence has to carry this message to her, and in the scene which follows she leaves him with the impression that she favours Berthold's proposal.

In the last Act of the play Berthold and Colombe meet to discuss this proposal. He offers no love, but the glory which he is confident his ambition will bring him. The courtiers, motivated by jealousy of Valence, enter and inform Berthold of what they imagine to be the long-standing affair between Colombe and Valence. Berthold has sufficient perception to be able to dismiss this suggestion, and he once more offers his hand to Colombe. Valence is called in, but before he reaches Colombe he is in-informed by Melchior, the prince's companion, that she has already accepted Berthold's proposal. Melchior's motive in doing this is to observe the reaction of Valence and discover if his apparent nobility is real or assumed. Valence makes the noble gesture and wishes them well, assuming that they love each other. Colombe thanks him and offers him a gift to mark her wedding. Valence asks for the redressal of the wrongs of Cleves, remembering, even in this moment of disappointment, the interests of his fellow townsmen. Confirmed in her idea of his noble spirit, Colombe offers him her love and the play ends with their renunciation of the world for love. They are joined by the boisterous and impressible Guibert, the only one of the courtiers capable of understanding their nobility. Berthold is left wearily to pursue his chosen course of ambition, confirmed by the lovers in his knowledge that he has not taken the noblest course.

In this play, as in all those which precede it, Browning is examining the relationship between the human mind and Truth, or the Ideal. The concern which both Valence and Colombe show for the interests of the people is a manifestation of their nobility of spirit. It is the same nobility of spirit which allows them to adopt without hesitation what they know to be the finest course. The courtiers are all governed by motives of self-interest, the mean and the trivial. The title of the play is significant; it is Colombe's birthday—the birthday of her soul as well as of her body. She realizes what Valence stands for:

> You know how love is incompatible
> With falsehood—purifies, assimilates
> All other passions to itself.

Act 5

Berthold is incapable of quite this degree of nobility. Melchior, who attends him out of a sense of respect for his qualities, knows that his nature is higher than he allows it to be, and Berthold proves him right in his understanding of the lovers and their withdrawal from the world to which he is committed. Behind the plot there is an assumption that nobility of spirit and actual life are incompatible. The lovers *withdraw* from the world, leaving it unchanged except by the demonstration of their nobility.

### 'LURIA'

*Colombe's Birthday* was written for the stage. *Luria*, which followed it, was not. Yet *Colombe's Birthday* has more in common with *Luria* than with *A Blot on the Scutcheon*. It shares with *Luria*, which was published in April 1846, a tendency towards a fullness of style, which, while Browning was writing for Macready, he was trying to avoid. It is partly because of this that these two plays are, as literature, if not as drama, more satisfying. There is one point in the action of *Colombe's Birthday* when there is an effect of clogging; this occurs in Act 4, when Valence, who is supposed to inform Colombe of Berthold's offer, launches instead into a 45-line speech in praise of Berthold. The idea behind it is presumably to create an impression of irony—Valence says what he would cheerfully hear denied. However, the speech has the unfortunate effect of distracting our attention from the situation in which he finds himself and delaying what we are most interested in—the reaction of Colombe herself to the proposal. But this is only one point. On the whole, the increased use of monologue and the lengthened dialogue produce a greater impression of motivation, which, in his earlier work, Browning sacrificed in the attempt to achieve a dramatic effect.

In this *Luria* is similar to *Colombe's Birthday*. The plot of the play is the simplest of all those Browning had written up to this time. Luria, the hero, is a Moor employed by Florence as leader of her armed forces in the war against Pisa. True Florentine policy, always treacherous, had dictated that before Luria had gained the victory which his ability as a commander had made inevitable, movements should have been made to prevent his becoming too powerful and thus threatening the security of the state. The play shows the naïve and trusting Luria whose character is modelled on that of Othello, at the point of victory. He is surrounded by spies. Branccio, the Secretary of State, has been taking evidence from the Florentine soldier displaced by Luria, and from Luria's own statements and actions, in order to feed the secret trial which is going on in Florence. Domizia, a Florentine lady whose family had been accused of treason and destroyed by the state, hopes to use Luria in order to effect her revenge. The state is aware of this and has placed her by him in order to provide itself with an excuse to act. The only faithful servant Luria has at the beginning of the play is his fellow Moor, Husain. Yet the course of the action sees all those around him forced to recognize nobility and perfect integrity in him.

Luria learns of the secret trial from the commander of the Pisan army, who hopes to persuade him to join Pisa against his adopted state. Luria rejects the offer and remains at his post. After the victory over Pisa, Branccio confirms what Tiburzio, the Pisan commander, had told him. Now Luria has Florence in his power, but instead of leading his victorious troops against those who were plotting to destroy him, he sends Branccio back to Florence and remains at his camp. At the end of the play Branccio and Tiburzio return from the city where they have pleaded Luria's innocence in his defence; but it is too late Rather than allow his life to continue to the detriment of Florence, he has taken poison, and dies surrounded by those who have been forced to acknowledge the superiority of his nature.

Luria's suicide was motivated neither by indecisiveness nor by fear. He knows that for Florence to commit herself either to his guilt or to his innocence will be to her harm. Throughout the play he is motivated by a love for the city and a concept of the devotion of the individual to the service of the state. As this becomes more and more apparent, all those around him, Tiburzio the Pisan commander, Puccio the displaced soldier, the clerk Jacopo, the lady Domizia—all these become to some extent transformed by his honesty and nobility, forgetting themselves and their own interests. It is significant that Browning chooses Florence as the background to his play, because that city has always been notorious for the political cunning of its statesmen and for the fact that sad experience had taught it the impossibility of combining statesmanship and trust. Luria is a Moor, like Othello, because that race has, since Shakespeare's play was written, always been thought of as natural, motivated by instinct and impulse rather than by thought. Luria's death completes the statement of the play. Not only is it an intrinsic part of the character as Browning presents him, but it is necessary in order to free him from any suggestion of cunning. His last action epitomizes the nobility of his whole life.

### 'THE SOUL'S TRAGEDY'

*Luria* was Browning's last play, but it was published in the same volume (number seven of *Bells and Pomegranates*), as a work which is interesting in several ways. *The Soul's Tragedy* makes a statement which is almost opposite to that involved in *Luria*—it depicts the break-down of the integrity of a 'noble' soul. It is also particularly interesting because the way in which it is constructed suggests the main reason why Browning failed to succeed fully as a dramatist. The division of *The Soul's Tragedy* into two parts, both of which consist of a *situation* and avoid action, either external or internal, is symptomatic of the

72

fact that Browning was not really interested in the techniques and subject matter of drama. The play's two parts are:

Act First, Being what was called the Poetry of Chiappino's Life; And Act Second, Its Prose.

As the sub-title suggests, the first Act is in verse, the second in prose. The idea behind the division is that in the first part Chiappino shows nobility of soul, and in the second, meanness.

The setting of the action is Faenza, some time in the sixteenth century. Chiappino is a violent rebel against the tyranny of the Provost, who rules the town. His friend, Luitolfo, who is engaged to the woman whom they both love, favours compromise as a method of helping the people. When the action begins Chiappino has just been banished from the city. Luitolfo goes to plead with the Provost on Chiappino's behalf. While he is gone Eulalia, his fiancée, makes clear to Chiappino why she has chosen Luitolfo and the former expresses his impatience at the temporizing of Luitolfo and the citizens. As he is doing so Luitolfo returns and tells them that, angered by the Provost's refusal to reprieve Chiappino, he has killed him and is being pursued. Chiappino rises to the occasion, assumes command and sends Luitolfo away in disguise. When the mob arrives he assumes responsibility for his friend's act. It is only then that he realizes that they have come not to avenge the Provost, who is not dead, but to bestow power on his assailant.

The second part sees the arrival of the Papal Nuncio, Ogniben, who has come to invest Chiappino as the new Provost. This prose section shows the temporizing of Chiappino, who, when the noble impulse is over, is unable to avoid being drawn into temptation. In spite of his declared principles, he agrees to assume absolute power, claiming the good of the people as his end. Meanwhile, Ogniben, who is well aware that Chiappino is attributed with the responsibility of having attacked the Provost, leads him, with cynical wisdom, to a position from which there is no withdrawing, before informing him that his appointment depends on the punishment of the Provost's assailant. It is at this moment that Luitolfo, who has remained disguised in the crowd, steps forwards and claims the act. Chiappino beats a hasty and undignified retreat. Ogniben's first words in the scene had implied the cynical attitude towards rebellion and impulsiveness which was his main characteristic:

I have seen three-and-twenty leaders of revolts.

Act 2

His last words are:

I have known *four*-and-twenty leaders of revolts.

The cynicism of this remark gives the implication of human weakness in the story of Chiappino wider reference. To Ogniben, Chiappino's moral fall is part of the normal course of events.

*A Soul's Tragedy* has considerable interest in itself. The character of Ogniben is one of Browning's most successful portraits of the wise rogue. It is also interesting that his achievement here, which is so considerable, is made in prose and not in verse. Yet what the work indicates when seen in relation to the plays is that Browning's interest and ability were not well adapted to stage drama. He possessed the power to create character, but he was not interested in depicting the movement of that character. His lack of interest in external action was not a serious handicap to him. He claimed to be interested primarily in character and only secondarily in action. Much good drama has been written from this point of view. Christopher Marlowe's *Dr. Faustus*, for example, is far more dramatic when the focal point is the character of the hero than it is when the hero is acting. Yet an examination of the last speech of Faustus is enough to indicate where Browning fails:

Ah, Faustus.
Now hast thou but one bare hour to live,
And then thou must be damn'd perpetually!
Stand still, you ever-moving spheres of heaven,
That time may cease, and midnight never come;

Fair Nature's eye, rise, rise again, and make
Perpetual day; or let this hour be but
A year, a month, a week, a natural day,
That Faustus may repent and save his soul!
*O lente, lente currite, noctis equi!*
The stars move still, time runs, the clock will strike,
The devil will come, and Faustus must be damn'd.

This speech suggests and contains the mounting terror of Faustus as he waits for the inevitable moment when his pact with the Devil reaches its term. It is dramatic as nothing in Browning's plays is dramatic, because it actually portrays the movement in the mind of the man who is speaking it. Faustus tells us that he is terrified, but the way in which he speaks makes us also feel his terror. Browning nowhere in his plays shows either this sheer poetic ability, or the interest in the development of action which might have compensated for it. The only exception is the character of Ogniben in *A Soul's Tragedy*. This sole exception points to the basic reason for his failure. Throughout the plays Browning was concerned to state the supremacy of moral absoluteness over moral relativity. He is always trying to show that nobility of soul is possible. As in the early poetry, he is concerned with ideas, rather than with reality. When he turned to reality, which he reached through character and situation, he succeeded in writing poems of the very highest quality. It was not in writing plays that his talents were best employed.

BROWNING'S ESCAPE FROM SPASMODICISM

One can hardly regret the time which Browning gave to writing for the stage. His early poetry was basically derivative in form, as in content. The influence of Shelley, Southey and Byron was strong. Not long after the publication of *Sordello*, a kind of poetry became fashionable which derived from the same sources and which had all the characteristics of Browning's early poems. The poetry of Alexander Smith, author of *A Life Drama*, and of James Bailey, author of *Festus*, became known as the chief

75

work in the 'Spasmodic School'. The reception was at first extremely good. One reviewer said of Smith:

> When, therefore, we say that Alexander Smith is a poet and a man of unmistakeable genius, we are giving praise beyond the reach of epithets. . . . He makes his Muse a harpsichord, whereon he plays fragments of melody, practising his hand till some great 'symphony of song' may be born within him.
>
> Review in the LEADER

Already, in 1830, Henry Taylor, in the preface to his poem, *Philippe Van Artvelde,* had attacked the formlessness of this kind of poetry and commented on the unjustified degree of attention which it paid to metaphor and simile at the expense of sense. Browning was probably influenced by Taylor's work when writing *Sordello,* but before he began to write plays, his work bore quite a strong resemblance to that of the Spasmodics. Spasmodic poetry dropped quite sharply in the estimation of the Victorian reading public after 1854. In that year an elaborate parody of the 'life dramas' of Smith and Bailey was published under the title of *Firmilian or The Student of Badajoz, A Spasmodic Tragedy.* The author, William Aytoun, preceded it by an apparently serious review in *Blackwood's Magazine,* where he said:

> It is, of course, utterly extravagant; but so are the whole of the writings of the Spasmodic School; and, in the eyes of a considerable body of modern critics, extravagance is regarded as a proof of extraordinary genius. . . . [The Spasmodic poets] are simply writing nonsense-verses; but they contrive, by blazing away whole rounds of metaphor, to mask their absolute poverty of thought, and to convey the impression that there must be something stupendous under so heavy a canopy of smoke.
>
> Review of FIRMILIAN

By the time *Firmilian* came out, Browning could no longer be classed as a Spasmodic poet by even the most careless reader. By this time some of his best and most disciplined work had been written. However, he must have appeared in 1840, as the author of *Paracelsus* and *Sordello*, to be moving towards the extremes of formlessness and extravagance which Aytoun was attacking. It was the discipline which his sustained attempt to write for the stage imposed on him that brought him away from the earlier mode of writing and allowed him to develop the dramatic monologue. After 1845, he was under the influence of Elizabeth Barrett—and her early poetry has something Spasmodic about it—by then, however, Browning had found himself. It may have been the influence of his wife which led him to produce the relatively unsuccessful poems *Christmas Eve* and *Easter Day* in 1850, but if so, the influence ended there.

# 3

# After 'Sordello': Browning's Recovery

The reception of *Sordello* must have been a blow to Browning, but if so, it was one from which he had every intention of recovering as quickly as possible. During the years which followed he made a sustained attempt to recover what literary standing he had lost. If his reputation in the literary world of London had declined, he was not without interesting and stimulating friends. Some of these he found in the society of the suburbs, where he enjoyed the company of men like Christopher Dowson and Alfred Domett. The latter in particular was a life-long friend and supporter of Browning's poetry. When Domett went to New Zealand, where he eventually became Prime Minister before his return to England, he corresponded regularly with Browning. Their friendship was celebrated in the poem *Waring,* which Browning wrote some time in 1842. The friendship with Thomas Carlyle was kept up, and as time went by, the poet made new friends in London, like the poets, Bryan Waller Proctor, Thomas Hood and Leigh Hunt. Eventually he was to meet John Kenyon and through him to become acquainted with Elizabeth Barrett. His association with Richard Hengest Horne led to his helping Horne in his preparation of *The New Spirit of the Age,* which, along with articles on Carlyle, Dickens, Wordsworth, and many other of the most prominent literary figures of the time, included an article on the author of *Paracelsus* and *Sordello.* This ended with a not inaccurate estimate of his work so far:

The poet may be considered the Columbus of an impossible

discovery. It is a promised land, spotted all over with disappointments, and yet most truly a land of promise, if ever so rich and rare a chaos can be developed into form and order by revision, and its southern fullness of tumultuous heart and scattered vineyards be ever reduced to given proportion, and wrought into a shape that will fit the average mental vision and harmonize with the more equable pulsations of mankind.

To fulfil the promise of his earlier work and to escape from obscurity and incoherence was the task which Browning must have set himself in the years which immediately followed the publication of *Sordello.*

All Browning's work at this time was published in the series *Bells and Pomegranates.* The fact that every one of the volumes in the series was paid for by the poet's father and published at his own expense shows that his standing with the literary public was not very high. In this series all the plays after *Strafford* appeared, but it also included in the first, third and seventh volumes, *Pippa Passes, Dramatic Lyrics,* and *Dramatic Romances and Lyrics.* It is in these volumes that we see the dramatic monologue emerging and Browning turning towards the shorter narrative poem. By the time that the series was complete, he must have had a more or less clear idea of the kind of poetry which he was to continue to write, and in which he was to excel.

The title of the series puzzled many contemporary readers. It is derived from the passage in *Exodus* xxviii, 33-4, where Moses is instructed as to the decoration of the garment in which the priest must be dressed to approach the altar:

> And beneath upon the hem of it, thou shalt make pomegranates of blue, and of purple, and of scarlet, round about the hem thereof; and bells of gold between them round about. A golden bell and a pomegranate, upon the hem of the robe round about.

Elizabeth Barrett's insistence on an explanation drew from Browning two comments. In October 1845 he wrote to her:

The Rabbis make Bells and Pomegranates symbolical of Pleasure and Profit, the gay and the grave, the Poetry and the Prose, Singing and Sermonising—such a mixture of effects as in the original hour (that is, quarter of an hour) of confidence and creation.

In the middle of Volume 8 of the series, before *A Soul's Tragedy* and after *Luria*, he wrote,

Here ends my first Series of 'Bells and Pomegranates': and I take the opportunity of explaining, in reply to enquiries, that I only meant by that title to indicate an endeavour towards something like an alternation, or mixture, of music with discoursing, sound with sense, poetry with thought; which looks too ambitious, thus expressed, so the symbol was preferred. It is little to the purpose, that such is actually one of the most familiar of the many Rabbinical (and Patristic) acceptations of the phrase; because I confess that, letting authority alone, I supposed the bare words, in such juxtaposition, would sufficiently convey the desired meaning. 'Faith and good works' is another fancy, for instance, and perhaps no easier to arrive at: yet Giotto placed a pomegranate fruit in the hands of Dante, and Raffael crowned his theology . . . with blossoms of the same; as if the Belari and Vasari would be sure to come after, and explain that it was merely 'a symbol of good works . . .'.

Exactly why Browning thought of the poems in the series as divided into those which were primarily pleasant and those which were primarily meaningful, it is not always easy for the modern reader to see. However, it was certainly not the plays which were in the former class. They were serious; and it is the shorter poems of the volumes, those to which the modern reader directs his attention first, that Browning thought of in this comparatively light-hearted way.

### 'PIPPA PASSES'

This dramatic poem, published in Volume 1 of *Bells and Pomegranates*, is an experiment with a new form. Unlike the plays which preceded and followed it, *Pippa Passes* did not aspire to the condition of drama. It consists of the juxtaposition of four dramatic incidents, connected only by the fact that Pippa herself is indirectly concerned in each of them. Pippa is a worker in the silk mill at Asolo. The poem begins with her song welcoming the first day of the New Year, which is a holiday for her, and during which she hopes to share the pleasure of others by imagining the happiness of their lives. In this way she thinks to obtain strength for the coming year:

> All other men and women that this earth
> Belongs to, who all days alike possess,
> Make general plenty cure particular dearth,
> Get more joy one way, if another, less:
> Thou art my single day, God lends to leaven
> What were all earth else, with a feel of heaven,—
> Sole light that helps me through the year, thy sun's!
>
> Introduction

Pippa chooses to think about those who seem to her the happiest four in Asolo. She hopes to realize, in turn, the happiness of Ottima, the object of the adulterous love of Sebald; the new-found love of the sculptor, Jules; the abiding love of Luigi's mother; and the divine love enjoyed by the Bishop. In imagining their happiness and importance, she indulges the fancy that, insignificant as she is, she will be as happy and important as they:

> And more of it, and more of it!—oh yes—
> I will pass each, and see their happiness,
> And envy none—being just as great, no doubt,
> Useful to men, and dear to God, as they!
>
> Introduction

What follows this introductory scene consists of a dramatic revelation of the real situation of each of these people whose happiness has been realized in Pippa's song. The reality is in ironic contrast to what the innocence of the singer had enabled her to imagine. Firstly we discover that dawn is bringing to

Ottima and her lover Sebald a terrible remorse. The corpse of her murdered husband lies where Sebald threw it the night before. Secondly, we hear the group of students, jealous of Jules's real ability, discussing the trick they have played on him. The innocent bride whom he is bringing home from the church, the young maiden whom he has wooed by letters, is, in fact, a prostitute. The students hide outside, waiting to see Jules's reaction when his bride, innocent of its meaning, recites the little piece which she has been made to learn by heart and which will reveal to her husband the trick which has been played. The moment comes and Jules reacts; coldly, he dismisses her. Thirdly, we witness a conversation between Luigi, a young patriot, and his mother. In the interval between the incidents, we have already learned that the Austrian secret police are watching Luigi. He has obtained a passport to leave Asolo. His intention is to go to Austria and kill an unnamed Austrian tyrant. The police, ignorant of this intention, suspect that he intends to use the passport to procure the safety of another patriot. If he does not leave at the appointed time they will be confirmed in their suspicions and will arrest him. Luigi's mother attempts to dissuade him from going on the journey. She fails to shake his certainty in the justice of his cause, but when she reminds him of the coming visit of Chiara—

> She must be grown—with her blue eyes upturned
> As if life were one long and sweet surprise:
> In June she comes . . .

3

—Luigi wavers.

The final incident involves the fate of Pippa herself. We know that there is a plot to harm her and that the villainous Englishman, Bluphocks, has been paid to seduce her. We leave her in the company of some factory girls, who are supposed to begin the process, and turn to the Bishop. He has recently come into his inheritance, after the death of his two elder brothers, and has received instructions from Rome to investigate allegations that the second brother, who had just died, had brought about the murder of the only child of the eldest brother. The steward of the second brother, in order to save himself from the results of his own villainy, reveals that the child is not dead, and identifies Pippa as the heiress. The temptation which he offers to the Bishop is merely to leave her where she is, assured of her moral degradation.

The turning point in all these incidents is the song of Pippa, heard from outside. Pippa's songs bring all the characters back to the right course of action at the crucial point. Finally, when she has brought Ottima and Sebald to face the consequences of what they have done, Jules to realize the spiritual purity of his bride, and Luigi to a renewed determination, Pippa is instrumental in enabling the Bishop to resist his temptation, and thus, unknowingly, assures herself of a happy future life. In the last scene we learn that she has avoided the temptation with which she was confronted, and is going to bed, completely unaware of the effect which she has had on those around her:

> Now, one thing I should really like to know:
> How near I ever might approach all these
> I only fancied being, this long day:
> —Approach, I mean, so as to touch them, so
> As to . . . in some way . . . move them—if you please,
> Do good or evil to them some slight way.
> For instance, if I wind
> Silk tomorrow, my silk may bind
> And border Ottima's cloak's hem.
> Ah me, and my important part with them,
> This morning's hymn half promised when I rose!
> True in some sense or other, I suppose.

4

The meaning of this poem has often been summarized by quotation of the words of Pippa's famous song:

> God's in his heaven,
> All's right with the world.                                  1

In fact, Pippa's other songs—about Kate the Queen; the wise

King; the dead child;—have as much claim to be taken as authoritative statements of Browning's doctrine. The statement of *Pippa Passes* is not to be found in any speech of Pippa's, but rather in the structure of the poem—in what is *done* rather than in what is *said*. If we take Pippa's voice as that of Browning, then the 'moral' of the poem would be—

> All service ranks the same with God—
> With God, whose puppets, best and worst,
> Are we: there is no last nor first.
>
> 4

However, this statement bears the same relationship to the action of the poem as does the final statement of the old seaman in Coleridge's *The Rime of the Ancient Mariner*:

> He prayeth best who loveth best
> All things both great and small;
> For the dear God who loveth us,
> He made and loveth all.
>
> 7, 614–617

This poem does carry this meaning, but it carries far more, which is conveyed through the complex structure of symbols and through its 'atmosphere'. *Pippa Passes* does support the conclusion of Pippa herself, but it is merely *her* conclusion, and the meaning which is conveyed in the action is of wider reference.

*Pippa Passes* demonstrates Browning's concern with the relationship between God and the world, and the balance in the world of good and evil. In each case, the impending catastrophe is averted by Pippa's song, which is the result of chance. Thus, the poem is *optimistic* rather than *realistic*, in so far as it puts forward a view of life which does not coincide with ordinary human experience. The avoidance of evil is felt by the reader not to be inevitable, because it does not grow out of the situation in each case, but is imposed on it from without. In each case, the reader is tempted to ask what would have happened if Pippa had *not* sung when and where she did. However, Browning is not in fact attempting to present some kind of explanation of evil, but is putting forward a favourite statement of his—

that good and evil are mixed in the world, but that the mixture does not result in a cancellation one of the other. The meaning of the poem is to be sought in the dramatic irony which arises because Pippa is so unaware either of the real nature of the circumstances of the people she imagines, or of the influence she has had on them. Her *unawareness* of the pattern which is revealed in the poem—the pattern which assures the predominance of good—is what Browning is concerned that we should appreciate. He would imply that our approach to the world is much the same—with the difference that we do not have her innocence of evil and purity of faith. By means of the poem we are brought beyond unawareness, to conceive of a pattern of action—by implication the pattern which exists in all action.

### LYRIC AND DRAMATIC

*Pippa Passes* contains a unique balance between lyrical and dramatic elements. In this context, 'lyrical' implies that the verse is of the type that attempts to bring about an emotional or intellectual state in the reader by means of its own rhythmic and verbal qualities; 'dramatic' suggests that the object of the writer has been to realize, in terms of speech and action, a character in relation to an object, an event, or another character. In verse which is 'lyrical' the language will convey the statement direct to the reader by means of his susceptibility to verse effects. In 'dramatic' verse, the language is not the primary object of attention, and the reader will be more aware of the explicit object of the language—that is, it will be concerned with dialogue or action. So used, the words must be kept clear of association with song or drama, though it is from them that they derive. Song may be used dramatically, as it is in *Pippa Passes* or *The Tempest,* and dramatic verse may be lyrical, as it is in Milton's *Comus.* The speech of Comus which describes the song of the Lady—

> Can any mortal mixture of Earth's mould
> Breathe such Divine inchanting ravishment?
> Sure something holy lodges in that breast,

And with these raptures moves the vocal air
To testifie his hidd'n residence;
How sweetly did they float upon the wings
Of silence, through the empty-vaulted night
At every fall smoothing the Raven down
Of darkness till it smil'd. . . .                           *244–252*

—is ostensibly a passage of dramatic verse, claiming to have
reference to the reaction of one character to the song of another.
In fact, it refers more to the song of the Lady than to Comus's
feelings about it. The real 'reason' for the passage is the description of the divine qualities of the song (and, by implication, of
the Lady herself). Comus becomes merely a stand-in for Milton,
who wishes to engineer our responses himself, rather than a
character whose reaction is dramatically interesting.

In *Pippa Passes*, there is a deliberate mixture of lyrical and
dramatic elements. The verse in the Ottima and Sebald incident
is dramatic, and the song of Pippa is lyrical. The poem is a
series of dramatic incidents within a lyrical context. This is
appropriate because Browning's conception of the work allows
for a distinction between the realistically described incidents,
in which good and evil are mixed, and the description of the
part which Pippa plays, which is not realistic. The mixture of
elements of verse and prose is only another indication of this
basic mixture of naturalistic, dramatic action, and stylized
description.

### DRAMATIC ROMANCES AND LYRICS
One poem in the two volumes of shorter poems which appeared
as Volumes 3 and 7 of *Bells and Pomegranates* is similar to
*Pippa Passes*, although it was written some two years later.
*In a Gondola* is structurally a drama, but stylistically a lyric.
The situation is dramatic and the form is that of a dialogue.
The dialogue takes place between two lovers in a gondola. At
the end of the poem the lovers leave the gondola, and as they
come ashore, the man is set upon and stabbed to death by the
brothers of the woman. However, the effect of the poem is not

86

to present an action so much as to make a lyrical statement of love. The action is merely the setting for this statement. Moving from present to past, the lovers give a history of their relationship and convey the sense of a highly sensual passion:

The moth's kiss, first!
Kiss me as if you made believe
You were not sure, this eve,
How my face, your flower, had pursed
Its petals up; so, here and there
You brush it, till I grow aware
Who wants me, and wide ope I burst.

The bee's kiss, now!
Kiss me as if you entered gay
My heart at some noon day,
A bud that dares not disallow
The claim, so all is rendered up,
And passively its shattered cup
Over your head to sleep I bow.

The fierceness and intensity with which this passion strives for an ultimate fulfilment, which mocks the finality of death, carries suggestions of destructiveness. Lines like these—

Now pluck a great blade of that ribbon-grass
To plait in where the foolish jewel was,
I flung away: since you have praised my hair,
'Tis proper to be choice in what I wear.

—contain an insistence on the super-eminence of love which prepares us for the lover's indifference to his own death.

The poem is an early treatment of a recurrent theme in Browning's work—that commitment to the truth of the emotions is sufficient to overcome even death. The theme was later to receive more didactic treatment in *The Statue and the Bust*, the story of lovers who failed to act and gave way to the pressure of circumstances. Browning's conclusion to this poem is:

Stake your counter as boldly every whit,
Venture as warily, use the same skill,
Do your best, whether winning or losing it,

If you choose to play!—is my principle.
Let a man contend to the uttermost
For his life's set prize, be it what it will!

The counter our lovers staked was lost
As surely as if it were lawful coin:
And the sin I impute to each frustrate ghost

Is—the unlit lamp and the ungirt loin, . . .

The statement of the two poems is similar. In both Browning implies that commitment to an object or ideal is the most important thing in life; in both, the object lies in the fulfilment of an emotional desire. On the other hand, the difference between the methods by which the two poems make that statement is an indication of the way in which Browning was developing during these years. In the six years between writing the two poems Browning finally moved away from the lyrical/dramatic form, and towards the dramatic monologue and narrative poem, in which we see his best and most characteristic work.

It is difficult to see from the present arrangement of the poems which originally belonged to the third and seventh volumes in *Bells and Pomegranates,* how Browning was developing at this time. The contents of the two volumes were later combined with those of the *Men and Women* volume and substantially rearranged for the collected edition of 1863. As originally published, Volume 3, *Dramatic Lyrics,* consisted of sixteen poems. Eleven of these were linked together in five groups. The principle on which Browning worked when making these groups seems to have been a vague one. *Cavalier Tunes* speak for themselves—they are bells rather than pomegranates, little more than exercises in metre. However, the grouping of the other poems is interesting in that it suggests that, at this time, Browning was unaware of the possibility of grouping the poems according to form rather than subject. Groups two and three are *Italy and France* and *Camp and Cloister*. The link in the first place is merely that both poems deal with attitudes towards women—in the one case, French, in the other, Italian. The connection between the poems in *Camp and Cloister* is the presence of a kind of emotion in the one which one would expect to find only in the other. The soldier in the one poem is motivated by a sense of self-sacrifice which contrasts with the malice and hatred of the monk in the other poem. In fact, the modern reader is struck by the fact that both *Italy*, which was later published as *My Last Duchess*, and *Cloister*, which later became *Soliloquy in the Spanish Cloister*, are dramatic monologues, in which the attention of the reader is directed primarily towards the character of the speaker.

*France*, which later became known as *Count Gismond*, is also in the form of the monologue, but it is one in which the reader is concerned more with the nature of the events which are being described by the speaker than with the character of the speaker. The poem is extremely interesting, not so much for its quality as because it is a comparatively crude example of Browning's interest in the idea of chivalrous combat. Some recent critics have tried to prove that Browning's intention was to suggest that the speaker was guilty of the immorality of which she had been accused. One has only to compare Browning's treatment of the idea of the combat with William Morris's treatment of it in *The Judgment of God*, to perceive the essential difference:

> 'Swerve to the left, son Roger', he said,
>     'When you catch his eyes through the helmet-slit,
> Swerve to the left, then out at his head,
>     And the Lord God give you joy of it!'

> The blue owls on my father's hood
>     Were a little dimm'd as I turn'd away;
> This giving up of blood for blood
>     Will finish here somehow today.

So—when I walk'd out from the tent,
    Their howling almost blinded me;
Yet for all that I was not bent
    By any shame. Hard by, the sea

Made a noise like the aspens where
    We did that wrong, but now the place
Is very pleasant, and the air
    Blows cool on any passers face. . . .

This Oliver is a right good knight,
    And must needs beat me, as I fear,
Unless I catch him in the fight,
    My father's crafty way—John, here!

Bring up the men from the south gate,
    To help me if I fall or win,
For even if I beat, their hate
    Will grow to more than this mere grin.

THE JUDGMENT OF GOD

The whole point of this poem is that the hero knows that he is going to fail because he knows that he is guilty. The tone of this poem is that of all Morris's work, which is pervaded by a sense of the futility of action. Browning, on the other hand, is concerned always to insist on the value of action, and this is why he uses the idea of the trial by combat, which assumes the influence of God in human action. Thus we see the idea again in *The Ring and the Book*, while *Before and After* is an analysis and justification of it.

*Count Gismond* is a monologue, but it can hardly be called a dramatic monologue in the sense of the term which is meant when some of the other poems in these volumes are referred to. *Soliloquy of the Spanish Cloister* and *My Last Duchess* are fully developed dramatic monologues because in them the attention of the reader is directed primarily and throughout the poem to the character of the speaker. Several of the other poems have much in common with these two, but in no other is the degree of attention which is paid to the character of the speaker predominant. In *Artemis Prologuizes* the personality of the speaker is merely formal. In *Rudel, Cristina* and *Waring,* the personal pronoun is depersonalized. The speaker's 'I' is no more than a convention which allows Browning to make a lyrical exposition of certain love-states, and, in the case of the third poem, *Waring,* to modify his concept of the hero. Even Waring himself is used in order to make a statement about the 'distinguished names' of the Victorian time.

*Johannes Agricola* and *Porphyria's Lover* can be grouped with *Soliloquy of the Spanish Cloister* because all three poems are studies of morbid psychology, but there are important formal differences. *Johannes Agricola,* for example, is almost purely lyrical in style. The poem portrays the state of belief (and indirectly the state of mind), of a religious fanatic. There is no objective realization of the individual concerned, and the reader's reception of the opinions expressed is a matter between the verse and himself. Any consideration which we may make about Johannes himself will be *deduced* from our thoughts concerning his belief and the fact that that belief is obsessional.

This is not the case with *Soliloquy of the Spanish Cloister.* Unlike most of Browning's later dramatic monologues, the poem has an obvious and strongly pronounced stanza form. Each stanza—for example:

> There's a great text in Galatians,
> > Once you trip on it, entails
> Twenty-nine distinct damnations,
> > One sure, if another fails:
> If I trip him just a-dying,
> > Sure of heaven as sure can be,
> Spin him round and send him flying
> > Off to hell, a Manichee?                7

—consists of eight lines of eight and seven syllables in alternation, rhyming regularly, *ababcdcd.* The lines are trochaic, but a glance at them will show the extent of the variation. Thus, in the first and fifth lines of the first stanza, the pause in the trochee is drawn out in such a way as almost to break the foot in two:

> Gr-gr-r—there/ go, my/ heart's ab/horrence!

> What? your/ myrtle/-bush wants/ trimming?

Other lines are more regular.

It is significant that it is only the name of Brother Lawrence that we hear—the speaker remains nameless. This suggests that the apparent purpose of the poem is the realization of Brother Lawrence. The actual end of the poem is the creation of the character of the speaker in relation to Brother Lawrence. We see Lawrence clearly through the eyes of the speaker, in terms of his care, neatness, love for his garden, natural behaviour and evident sanctity. Through the innocence which prevents him from suspecting what is wrong with his plants, the straight-forwardness with which he drains his watered orange pulp, we see the malice and hypocrisy of the speaker. Even the accusation of lustfulness reflects back against the man who is making it:

> —Can't I see his dead eye glow,
> Bright as t'were a Barbary corsair's?
> (That is, if he'd let it show!)　　　　　　　　4

The fact that the speaker describes Brother Lawrence's eye as 'dead', in spite of his desire that it should not be, gives the lie to his accusation. The effect of the whole poem is to give us a vivid impression of the psychology of malice. The way in which the verse form is manipulated adds to this impression. The regularity of the form, persistently being slowed down and speeded up by the speaker, gives an impression of constrained passion, brought to a final illustration in the last two lines:

> 'St, there's Vespers! *Plena gratiâ*
> *Ave, Virgo!* Gr-r-r—you swine!　　　　　　　9

In *Soliloquy of the Spanish Cloister* we see one of Browning's first studies of the comic rogue. *My Last Duchess* is more serious. As DeVane points out, this is the first attempt at portraying characters of Renaissance Italy—the setting which was to provide so many of the characters in the *Men and Women* volume. It is rather ironical that the poem should have grown out of the studies for *Sordello*, as seems to have been the case. *My Last Duchess* is the first poem which confirms the tendencies shown elsewhere in this volume and marks the final departure from the old manner.

The situation in this poem is fully explained only at the end. The speaker, a Duke, is taking round his picture gallery an emissary from the Count for the hand of whose daughter he is in negotiation. Consequently, our knowledge of the situation is cumulative and gathers strength with our growing knowledge of the character of the speaker. The poem is truly dramatic. The immediate aim of the Duke is to explain to the emissary the fault of his last Duchess, and so make a grim warning as to what he expects of his bride. Browning's purpose in creating the Duke is to make a statement about the comparative values of sophistication and naturalness. In this the use of the picture is important. The portrait is that of the dead woman who was last married to the Duke. He stops before it and unveils it for the benefit of the emissary. The contrast between the picture and the person whom it represents is that between Art and Life. The Duchess herself was too much aware of being alive:

> Sir, 'twas all one! My favour at her breast,
> The dropping of the daylight in the West,
> The bough of cherries some officious fool
> Broke in the orchard for her, the white mule
> She rode with round the terrace—all and each
> Would draw from her alike the approving speech,
> Or blush, at least.

Her 'depth and passion' were acceptable to the Duke only when modified by sophisticated convention. His pride in his nobility prevented him from asking her for what he wanted, so—

> . . . I gave commands;
> Then all smiles stopped together. There she stands
> As if alive.

This last line is a repetition of the opening line of the poem—

> That's my last Duchess painted on the wall,
> Looking as if she were alive.

For this picture the Duke has respect. He calls it a wonder. Likewise the statue of Neptune 'taming a sea-horse', which is a 'rarity'. It is only as Art that the Duke can accept the 'depth and passion'. Life is beyond him.

It was with poems as disciplined and concise as *My Last Duchess* that Browning gradually won back the audience which he had lost with *Sordello*. Yet the shorter poems of *Bells and Pomegranates* were not what Browning relied on to effect this end. At this time his hopes were directed rather towards the drama, and the series as originally projected did not allow for the publication of the shorter poems at all. In fact, one can see, in the way in which the poems are arranged, that Browning was, at this stage, unaware of the direction in which he was developing. By the time that he re-grouped the poems in 1863, he understood what had been happening, and acted accordingly. However, in 1846, when he brought the series to an end, he had other things to think about—things which kept him occupied for some time to come.

# 4

# New Developments: from Marriage to 'Men and Women'

On 12 September 1846, almost exactly five months after the conclusion of the *Bells and Pomegranates* series, Robert Browning and Elizabeth Barrett were secretly married in a London church. Browning was thirty-four, Elizabeth Barrett forty. After the marriage the bride returned to her father's house, where she remained for a week. Then, without informing her family, she left the house in Wimpole Street and accompanied her husband to Italy.

This was the culmination of a courtship which had lasted since January 1845. The poets had begun to correspond as a result of their mutual friendship with John Kenyon. Elizabeth Barrett knew Browning's work before she knew him, and thought highly of it. She had been writing and publishing poetry since she was fourteen, though the most important of her works written before she met Browning was the volume containing *A Drama of Exile*, published in 1844. Miss Barrett shared with Browning an extremely high conception of the function of the poet, an interest in the medieval, and a tendency towards the sublime and transcendent in her poetry. Unlike her husband, she was not physically active. While he was moving more than ever in the social world and had just been to Italy for the second time when they met, she had been an invalid for a number of years, confined to her room, more often than not in semi-darkness.

Exactly what was wrong with Elizabeth Barrett has never been established. Accounts of her illness vary—according to some it was a spinal injury, according to others a blood disease, and according to a small minority it was self-induced as a result of her neurotic sense of responsibility for her brother's death. Her brother Edward had been visiting her at the seaside where she was convalescing. The prearranged term of his visit had come, but she wrote to their father asking for permission for Edward to remain. The permission was grudgingly given; he stayed, went yachting on a clear day, and was drowned. Even years later she could hardly bring herself to mention the subject. However, she had been an invalid for some time before this event, and, whatever the reason for her illness, it seems to have been genuine enough. The situation in her family did not help. Her father, Edward Moulton Barrett, was a domestic tyrant of the worst kind. His jealousy of his family amounted to a mania and he opposed the marriage of even his fully-grown sons. The relationship between Elizabeth and her father was particularly close, and this was all the more reason for there being no chance of his ever consenting to her marriage—or allowing it to take place. Nor, until Robert Browning arrived on the scene, did there appear any chance of her meeting anyone to marry. She had a large circle of friends to whom she wrote regularly, but whom she rarely saw. It must have been as an addition to this circle that she thought of him—that is, until the morning after the afternoon on which he had been allowed to see her for the first time. That morning brought a letter containing a passionate declaration of love. Elizabeth returned it, asking Browning to burn it. He replied apologetically, and the relationship settled down into a steady pattern of courtship. The two poets had plenty in common. They differed on few points; she was more emotional in her judgments, and more liable to be deceived; he had a tendency towards coarseness of thought which she objected to—his attitude towards the duel was the one subject on which serious disagreement occurred during their courtship. But they were both prepared to adjust to each other and the long correspondence gave them plenty of opportunity. In the end, matters were brought to a head by the stupidity and obstinacy of Edward Barrett. Elizabeth had been recommended by various doctors to spend the winter in Italy. There were schemes afoot for her to be accompanied there by perfectly respectable female friends. Suddenly her father decided that she should not go. Her friends were horrified at the danger to her health. The lovers were forced to act when they did by her father's decision to take the family out of town while the house was being re-decorated. Browning stepped in and the secret marriage took place.

The Brownings did not start their married life with very much money. His father had given him £100, and she had an income of about £300. This was all they had for the first few years of married life in Florence, where their son was born in 1849. Then, in 1856 occurred the death of John Kenyon, their mutual friend, who left them £11,000 between them. During these years Browning was not active. Apart from *Christmas Eve* and *Easter Day,* which were published in April 1850, he published nothing between 1846 and November 1855, when *Men and Women* came out. Instead of writing he turned his attention to drawing and sculpting. Even after *Men and Women,* nothing further was produced until *Dramatis Personae,* in 1865. During the same period of time, Elizabeth Browning finished her *Sonnets from the Portuguese,* published her *Poems* in 1850 and *Casa Guidi Windows* in 1851. 1860 saw the appearance of her *Poems before Congress,* and in between this and *Casa Guidi Windows* she found time to write her 11,000-line narrative and discursive poem, *Aurora Leigh.*

Obviously, marriage was good for Elizabeth's Muse, if not for her husband's. He produced less during this period of twenty years than at any other time in his life. Yet what he produced was his best work. The poems in the volumes which came out in 1855 and 1865 are comparable only with the poem which followed them, *The Ring and the Book.* One can think of several possible reasons for this long period of comparative silence. The influence of his wife and her work, which was far more declamatory than his own, may have led him to suspect that he was losing sight of his true object as a poet. The death of his mother in 1849 (one week after the birth of his son), threw him into a depression which lasted for months and may have had some effect on his ability to write. Then again, it is possible that the process of drastic re-thinking which occurred in England during these years on religious and philosophical subjects, caused him some concern about the relationship between his poetry and the contemporary situation. The only thing which we have any real evidence for is a degree of formal uncertainty which seems to have persisted throughout the period. Looking at the list of the poems which he published at this time, one is led to think that Browning was uncertain about the kind of poetry which he wanted to write.

By 1863 when Browning came to revise his poems for the *Collected Edition*, he showed in his rearrangement that he recognized the development which had taken place in his career and the emergence of several clearly-defined types of poems, among which the dramatic monologue was the most prominent. To concentrate on this type of poem alone would give an inaccurate idea of Browning's development at this time and an insufficient impression of the extent of his poetic achievement. It is obviously impossible to examine many of the poems here. Instead, one or two poems from each group are taken as representative, in order to bring out the nature of Browning's preoccupations and the technical brilliance of his work, during this period.


'THE FLIGHT OF THE DUCHESS': A DRAMATIC NARRATIVE

We have information from Browning about the composition of this poem. He wrote, in 1883, to Doctor Furnival, the founder of the Browning Society, telling him how an interruption while he was composing the poem broke his train of thought and led him, when asked for a poem by the assistant editor of *Hood's Magazine*, to submit it in an incomplete state, consisting only of stanzas 1–9. He continued:

Some time afterwards I was staying at Bettisfield Park, in Wales, and a guest, speaking of early winter, said 'the deer had already to break the ice in the pond'. A fancy struck me, which, on returning home, I worked up into what concludes the story—which originally all grew out of this one intelligible line of a song that I heard a woman singing at a bon-fire Guy Faux night when I was a boy—*Following the Queen of the Gypsies, O!*

He also made an interesting communication to Elizabeth Barrett in July 1845:

> . . . as I conceived the poem, it consisted entirely of the Gypsy's description of the life the Lady was to lead with her future Gypsy lover—a *real* life, not an unreal one like that with the Duke. And as I meant to write it, all their wild adventures would have come out and the insignificance of the former vegetation have been deducible only—as the main subject has become now; of course it comes to the same thing, for one would never show half by half like a cut orange.

These two passages are interesting in themselves, as showing something of the method of composition which Browning followed. But they also provide an interesting commentary on the form of the poem as it *was* written. That Browning chose to tell the story as he did, dealing directly with the vegetation, and only implying the romantic life which was to follow, means that the poem became much more complex than it was when first conceived.

The basic point which Browning is making in the poem would have been made whichever way he had told it—that life without any kind of emotional engagement is unreal, life with love and romance, real. By telling the story of the girl's life with the young Duke and his mother in detail, he also allows himself to achieve an extension of the comment through the Duke's pathetic attempt to ape the medieval. It is important that he chooses to tell the story through the mouth of a servant:

> You're my friend:
>     I was the man the Duke spoke to;
> I helped the Duchess to cast off his yoke, too;

So here's the tale from beginning to end,
My friend!

THE FLIGHT OF THE DUCHESS I

By this means a direct connection is made possible between the immediate past of the late Duke, the young man's father, and the present of the young Duke himself. The servant, admiring the father, and despising the son, is able to bring out this contrast with considerable effect, stressing also the essentially *natural* background to the story:

> Ours is a great wild country:
>   If you climb to our castle's top,
>   I don't see where your eye can stop;
> For when you've passed the cornfield country,
> Where vineyards leave off, flocks are packed,
> And sheep-range leads to cattle-tract,
> And cattle-tract to open-chase,
> And open-chase to the very base
> Of the mountain. . . .
> Down the other side again
>   To another greater, wilder country,
> That's one vast red drear burnt-up plain . . .
>   And so on, more and ever more,
> Till at the last, for a bounding belt,
>   Comes the salt sand hoar of the great sea-shore,
>   And the whole is our Duke's country.                    2

Against this background stands forth the artificiality which killed the old Duke and ruined his son.

Faced with the artificiality and anti-natural attitude of the young Duke and his mother (based on vanity and supported by malice), the young bride who is brought to the castle can do nothing. She pines away, little by little, until her freedom comes with the Gypsies. They too are natural; they come from the ground:

> . . . with us, I believe they rise out of the ground,
> And nowhere else, I take it, are found
> With the earth-tint yet so freshly embrowned. . . .        8

The old woman, the Queen of the Gypsies, who brings freedom to the Duchess, is like the image of Death; the Duke takes her as such:

> He was contrasting, 'twas plain from his gesture,
> The life of the lady so flower-like and delicate,
> With the loathsome squalour of this helicat.          8

This mistake which the young Duke makes is to assess the old woman too simply in terms of appearances and to make too sophisticated an estimation of his young wife. The old woman has within her a mysterious natural power; she offers the Duchess freedom, giving her a vision of a life of emotional fulfilment, a life which is natural in its beginning as in its end:

> So, at the last shall come old age,
> Decrepit as befits that stage . . .
> And then as, 'mid the dark, a gleam
>     Of yet another morning breaks,
> And like the hand which ends a dream,
> Death, with the might of his sunbeam,
>     Touches the flesh and the soul awakes,
> Then— . . .          15

Our sense of the importance of the girl's acceptance of this life is increased by our apprehension of the character of the narrator. His reluctance to trust the Gypsy woman emphasizes the power of the force which compels him to admit that the Duchess's choice is the right one. His own love for Jacynth, the Duchess's maid, heightens our sense of the impact which the transformation of the Duchess has on him:

> . . . I stopped as if struck by palsy.
> She was so different, happy and beautiful,
> I felt at once that all was best,
> And that I had nothing to do, for the rest,
> But wait her commands, obey and be dutiful. . . .
>     I saw the glory of her eye,
> And the brow's height and the breast's expanding,
>     And I was hers to live or to die.          15

It is through his yearning after the Duchess and the glimpse
of a higher kind of life which he has had, that we feel most
strongly the attraction of the life to which she has gone. Like
the ballad which was the source of Browning's inspiration, his
poem resists the temptation to be specific. The ballad gives no
details about the kind of life which the lady is to live:

> There were three gypsies a-come to my door,
> And down-stairs ran this lady, O!
> One sang high and another sang low
> And the other sang bonny bonny Biscay O!
>
> Then she pull'd off her silk finished gown
> And put on hose of leather, O!
> The ragged ragged rags about our door,
> She's gone off with the wraggle taggle gypsies O!
>
> THE GYPSY LADDIE, Anon.

Where the ballad concentrates on the moment of the lady's
rejection of civilized finery, Browning's poem stresses the
way in which the narrator is tied to the Duke by a principle
of loyalty which belonged to the natural order as he knew it,
giving him, throughout his life, the yearning desire to seek for
his lady. Because he is bound by the ties of life as he conceives
of them, he is unable to escape with the lady—he cannot understand the song of the Gypsy. But at the end of his life, when
those ties have faded away, he nourishes the dream of freedom
to live a completely natural life—and to meet a completely
natural death. In a way, the narrator is the reader; like the
reader, he is bound within the circle of ordinary perception;
like the reader, he sees the attraction of what lies beyond. The
young Duchess has made the journey from ordinary life to
freedom—to a life where love and nature are the conditions of
existence.

'CHILDE ROLAND TO THE DARK TOWER CAME':
A DRAMATIC SITUATION IN NARRATIVE
In *The Flight of the Duchess* Browning uses the same device of

the feminine irregular rhyme (delicate/helicat), which he used in *Christmas Eve* and *Easter Day*. In the latter poems he used it to achieve an impression of humour which is not so successful as the impression of scorn which it gives to the servant in the former poem. In *The Flight of the Duchess*, that suggestion, supported by skilful construction and a careful distancing of his subject by means of the servant's age, helps him to effect a strong sense of the opposition between romantic reality and the false reality of sophistication. If anything, *Childe Roland to the Dark Tower Came* is even more successful in creating a romantic atmosphere, though to a different end. The title of the poem is taken from a line in Edgar's song in *King Lear*:

> Childe Rowland to the dark tower came,
> His word was still,—Fie, foh, and fum,
>     I smell the blood of a British man.

KING LEAR 3, 5

In its context in *King Lear* the line has no apparent meaning, but is mysterious and suggestive. Browning takes this strangely emotive line, and builds around it a specific, concrete context. He puts both Childe Roland and the Dark Tower in the context of the chivalric quest—a theme which was, throughout his career, a convenient and attractive medium for the expression of his philosophy.

Like *The Flight of the Duchess*, this poem, though primarily narrative, has strong dramatic elements. Childe Roland's situation is highly dramatized, from the first moment when he speaks to the old man (who seems to owe something to the mysterious old man in Chaucer's *Pardoner's Tale*):

> My first thought was, he lied in every word,
>     That hoary cripple, with malicious eye
>     Askance to watch the working of his lie
> On mine, and mouth scarce able to afford
> Suppression of the glee, that pursed and scored
> Its edge, at one more victim gained thereby.

CHILDE ROLAND I

103

This first stanza sets the tone of the whole poem. It is noticeable that we are told remarkably little in this passage apart from the physical appearance of the old man, and the effect which it had on the Knight. We do not yet know that the Knight has asked for direction; nor do we know anything about the quest which he is on. Only gradually do we learn that the Knight is dedicated to search for the Dark Tower and that many set out with him but failed along the way. He is now the sole survivor of those who began the quest many years before.

The tone of the poem is strengthened by the description of the scenery. It is important to notice that there is no suggestion of the supernatural and that Browning achieves the very strong sense of horror which the poem contains only by putting natural objects in a certain light—the weeds, the lack of animal and other vegetable life, the old horse; all these things are only what we might expect to find elsewhere. The accumulation gives each one a powerful effect, so that the river, ordinary enough in itself, becomes, in the context, a thing of horror:

> A sudden little river crossed my path
>   As unexpected as a serpent comes.
>   No sluggish tide congenial to the glooms;
> This, as it frothed by, might have been a bath
> For the fiend's glowing hoof—to see the wrath
>   Of its black eddy bespate with flakes and spumes.
>
> So petty yet so spiteful! All along,
>   Low scrubby alders kneeled down over it;
>   Drenched willows flung them headlong in a fit
> Of mute despair, a suicidal throng:
> The river which had done them all the wrong,
>   What e'er that was, rolled by, deterred no whit.          19, 20

This passage is an extended example of the pathetic fallacy—the attribution to inanimate objects of the feelings of human beings. It is also interesting to notice that the description of the river—as of the waste land throughout the poem—would be applicable to any similar scene in an area made barren by over-industrialization. It is reminiscent of the treatment of certain urban areas in the novels of Dickens.

The transformation of this landscape into a setting suggestive of horror is brought about partly by putting it into the context of the knightly quest. It is interesting to see something of the same kind of thing being done by Auden, in his poem *The Three Companions*, in which he adapted the form of the popular medieval poem, *The Cutty Wren*:

> 'O where are you going?' said reader to rider,
> 'That valley is fatal when furnaces burn,
> Yonder's the midden whose odours will madden,
> That gap is the grave where the tall return.'
>
> THE THREE COMPANIONS

But Auden does no more than exploit the suggestiveness of the idea for the purpose of making a statement about action. Browning draws out his waste land, relating it in detail to the psychology of the Knight, relating the diseased landscape to the mind overclouded with the idea of failure:

> Now patches where some leanness of the soil's
> Broke into moss or substances like boils;
> Then came some palsied oak. . . .                        26

Browning's description is close at times to that which is found in a poem by his wife, which she included in her volume of poems published in 1844:

> . . . the fourth pool and the last,
> Where weights of shadow were downcast
>
> From yew and alder and rank trails
> Of nightshade clasping the trunk-scales
> And flung across the intervals
>
> From yew to yew: who dares to stoop
> Where those dank branches overdroop,
> Into his heart the chill strikes up;

He hears a silent gliding coil,
The snakes strain hard against the soil,
His foot slips in their slimy oil,

And toads seem crawling on his hand,
And clinging bats but dimly scanned
Full in his face their wings expand.

A VISION OF POETS 164–177

In this passage there is all the usual paraphernalia of horror—
yew, nightshade, bats and toads, but there is no real success
in the attempt to convey it. Browning's poem has less of the
obviously horrible; (Childe Roland does not have to drink of
the river as the hero of Mrs. Browning's poem has to drink from
the pool). Yet Browning's poem succeeds just where his wife's
fails.

The reason for this success is to be found in the relationship
between the mind of the Knight and the situation in which he
finds himself. Thus, the sense of menace comes to a pitch in the
vision of hills, which appear firstly as animals locked in struggle,
and then as giants 'at a hunting'. Yet this horror, the sense of
failure which dominates the mind of the Knight as he waits for
what is to come and reviews the failure of those who set out
with him on the quest, only serves to stress his determination.
At the end of the poem—

Dauntless the slug-horn to my lips I set,
    And blew. *'Childe Roland to the Dark Tower came.'*      34

From out of the horror and menace and the sense of failure
there comes action—the final act of chivalric self-dedication. The
attempt is made; action is vindicated.

'SAUL': A LYRICAL NARRATIVE

Like *The Flight of the Duchess, Saul* was written in two stages.
The first 102 lines, up to the end of section 9, were written in
1845 and published in *Bells and Pomegranates*. In *Men and
Women*, the poem appeared with additional matter which made

it 239 lines long. Like the other poems in these volumes, it contains a strong element of drama in the situation of David before the giant Saul, twisted in statuesque agony, but is primarily lyrical. The dramatic situation provides a framework into which the songs of David can be fitted; the verse form—rhymed couplets consisting of five anapaestic feet, as in—

I have gone/ the whole round/ of crea/ tion: I saw/ and I spoke:

—is suited to song rather than narrative.

The basic source of the poem is in the passage in *Samuel* 1, xvi, 14–23, which concludes—

And it came to pass when the evil spirit from God was upon Saul, that David took an harp, and played with his hand: so Saul was refreshed, and was well, and the evil spirit departed from him.

It seems that Browning got the idea of writing a poem on the situation from his reading of the work of the eighteenth-century poet, Christopher Smart, who had written a lyrical poem in praise of God, called *The Song of David*. But Browning, in his expansion of his poem, made it a vehicle for the statement about the relationship between the perfection of God and the imperfection of His creation. The statement is dramatically relevant to the situation because it provides a lyrical assertion of faith to counterbalance the depression of the King.

*Saul* has in common with the two other poems discussed in this section so far, as well as the great majority of the poems written at this period, the exploitation of a dramatic situation to make a didactic statement. The situation, as often in Browning's work, is one marked by an absence of any encouraging faith, where action or striving after God seems impossible and pointless. The poem brings the reader, as it brings Saul, to the conviction that action is possible and that God is within reach. *Childe Roland* and *The Flight of the Duchess* do essentially the same thing, except that they do it more in terms of drama and narrative. The attempt to bring certainty out of uncertainty was the major poetic object of Browning and the reason for his fondness for themes of chivalry and the Andromeda myth, referred to in *Pauline* and depicted in the picture by Michelangelo da Caravaggio (1569–1609), an engraving of which he kept with him for many years. It was on the subject of the treatment of the medieval that he differed from Tennyson, as we see in a letter which he wrote in 1870:

> We look at the object of art in poetry so differently! Here is an Idyll about a knight being untrue to his friend and yielding to the temptation of that friend's mistress after having engaged to assist him in his suit. I should judge the conflict in the knight's soul the proper subject to describe: Tennyson thinks he should describe the castle, and the effect of the moon on its towers, and anything *but* the soul.
>
> To Miss Blagden

In this connection it is interesting to compare with Browning's the medieval poems of Dante Gabriel Rossetti, who was influenced by both Browning and Tennyson. Rossetti creates the atmosphere of the medieval in order to explore the relationship between the sensual and the ideal in human love. Browning tends always to avoid the emotional complexity which it is Rossetti's immediate aim to achieve. The result is that he sometimes tends to become over-positive in poems like *Count Gismond,* even when he does not fall into the temptation of preaching. In *Saul* he manages to avoid the temptation, and the type of situation which he created does not allow him to become over-positive. In the dramatic monologue he found a form which, for the time being, allowed a minimization of both dangers. Unfortunately, it was only for a time.

THE DRAMATIC MONOLOGUE

The dramatic monologue allowed Browning to exploit all his capacity for creating character, by means of his acute awareness of sounds and the associations of words, and thus to make his statement indirectly. In an examination of *Soliloquy of the*

*Spanish Cloister* and *My Last Duchess* it becomes apparent how he was able to imply the nature of the speakers by means of their reaction to something outside themselves. *My Last Duchess* also shows how he was able to make a more general statement of the moral attitudes and values of the Duke as shown in his speech—in the way in which he explained his requirements with regard to the marriage proposal which was being made to him. In the later dramatic monologue this ability is even more obvious. In *Fra Lippo Lippi* and *Karshish*, two poems which work in rather different ways, we see the extent to which his control over the dramatic monologue had developed.

KARSHISH'

In this poem, its full title being, *An Epistle Containing the Strange Medical Experience of Karshish, the Arab Physician*, it is relatively easy to see how Browning went about the process of creating the monologue. The very first lines of the poem, with their involved construction, their parenthetic comment on the nature of man (relating to the Platonic division of the soul and the flesh), create an impression of the scholar and the philosopher. The suggestions here of devotion to science, the humility and the piety and the formal structure are all shown in the rest of the poem to be basic to the character of the man. The form of the poem is that of a report on progress to a medical superior. The humour is professional:

> This Bethany, lies scarce the distance thence
> A man with plague-sores at the third degree
> Runs till he drops down dead. Thou laughest here!

The similes that come into his mind are scientific:

> As saffron tingeth flesh, blood, bones and all!

This is a man who examines life and natural phenomena with a dispassionate eye. So he examines the experience of Lazarus, who the Jewish elders claim was raised from the dead. To

Karshish the story is ridiculous—impossible. All his training and inclinations conspire to make him dismiss it. This he struggles to do. He is himself a religious man to whom the earthquake which accompanied the death of Christ was an omen of the death of his own 'lord' the sage; he tells Ahib that Christ died—

> . . . when the earthquake fell
> (Prefiguring, as soon appeared, the loss
> To occult learning in our lord the sage
> Who lived there in the pyramid alone). . . .

It is because he is so religious after his own fashion that he reacts so strongly to the suggestion of Christ's Divinity, hardly able to state a proposition which appears to him so blasphemous:

> This man so cured regards the curer, then,
> As—God forgive me! who but God himself,
> Creator and sustainer of the world,
> That came and dwelt in flesh on it a-while!
> —'Sayeth that such an one was born and lived, . . .
> Then died, with Lazarus by, for aught I know,
> And yet was . . . what I said nor choose repeat. . . .

All his basic principles encourage him to interpret the situation in terms of medicine and madness. To him Christ appears as 'the learned leech', Lazarus as 'the madman'. Persistently he makes attempts to thrust the idea out of his head, apologizing to Ahib for retailing such a trivial matter to him and excusing himself by stating his doubt that his Syrian messenger will deliver the message at all.

On the other hand, that training moves him to give a thorough account of the state of mind in which he finds Lazarus. His diagnosis of such a state, in which the subject manifests an entire indifference to all those things which the normal man finds most absorbing, is simple. Lazarus is as if reduced to a state of imbecility. Yet he is not apathetic, and the evidence of his love—

> ... he loves both old and young,
> Able and weak, affects the very brutes
> And birds—how say I? flowers of the field—
> As a wise workman recognizes tools
> In a master's workshop, loving what they make.

—combines with his impatience at ignorance and carelessness and sin, to insist on the possibility of the alternative explanation —that Lazarus, unable to forget the world of the spirit, lives in a state of perfect realization of the imperfection of the world of the flesh.

The strength of Karshish's resistance to this explanation— to the whole idea of there being anything unusual in the situation which has confronted him in this insignificant little Jewish town, creates the strength of the impression that he *cannot* in fact resist. Towards the end of the letter he once more throws off the sense of conviction and enlightenment which has been growing on him:

> Thy pardon for this long and tedious case,
> Which, now that I review it, needs must seem
> Unduly dwelt on, prolixly set forth!
> Nor I myself discern in what is writ
> Good cause for the peculiar interest
> And awe indeed this man hath touched me with.

This attempt and the persistent apology, the insistence on the unlikeliness of the letter reaching its destination and the unimportance of the whole affair—all reinforce the final bursting out of compulsive and confused realization at the end. Karshish is not convinced. For him, because of the bias of his whole character, conviction was impossible. For him Lazarus remains the 'madman'. But for us, to whom Browning has given the power to make an objective estimation of the total situation, our very sympathy with the Arab physician who struggles for truth in his own way, makes conviction come with the pathos of his compulsive exclamation at the possibility of a truth which he cannot quite accept:

The very God! think, Ahib; dost thou think?
So, the All-Great, were the All-Loving too—

'FRA LIPPO LIPPI'
This poem has always been one of the most popular of Browning's monologues. The subject, the Renaissance painter, Brother Lippi, is taken as one of the first painters in the naturalistic school, being made to voice many of Browning's convictions about Art and its relationship to reality and the Ideal. This insistence in the poem on the portrayal of the Real as a primary object, leaving the Ideal to be suggested or implied, indicates the basic change of emphasis which had come about in Browning's thoughts about Art—a change in which the shift from the shapeless, lyrical poems of the first phase had led to the evolution of the dramatic monologue, based on an awareness of natural speech patterns and rhythms.

Although Fra Lippo is made to echo the ideas of his creator, there is no suggestion of didacticism in the poem. It works in a rather different way to *Karshish*. In that poem Browning was concerned with giving force to his concept of the relation between the spiritual and the worldly by depicting it at two removes. We saw first the character of Karshish and through him the situation of Lazarus. In *Fra Lippo Lippi* the method is more direct. We are drawn to the statement by the attractiveness of the character; the vivid appreciation of life, which Lippo says is an essential pre-requisite for Art, is conveyed not merely by statement, but by demonstration.

As usual Browning begins the poem with the suggestion of a dramatic situation. Lippo has been seized by the night watch as he makes his way back to the palace of the Medici after an amorous escapade. The violence and extravagance of his vocabulary immediately suggest his character—'clap', 'Zooks', 'harry out', 'gullet's gripe'. The ideas which occur to him in the immediacy of the situation are strikingly vivid:

> . . . harry out, if you must show your zeal,
> Whatever rat, there, haps on his wrong hole,

And nip each softling of a wee white mouse,
*Weke, weke,* that's crept to keep him company!

. . . the house that caps the corner . . .

Zooks, are we pilchards, that they sweep the streets . . .?

In the first of these passages the '*Weke, weke*' is a touch included merely to add vitality to the described situation—the extra dimension of concrete life.

The excuses which Fra Lippo makes for himself are convincing:

I was a baby when my mother died
And father died and left me in the street.
I starved there, God knows how, a year or two
On fig-skins, melon-parings, rinds and shucks,
Refuse and rubbish. One fine frosty day,
My stomach being empty as your hat,
The wind doubled me up and down I went.
Old Aunt Lapaccia trussed me with one hand,
(Its fellow was a stinger as I knew)
And so along the wall, over the bridge,
By the straight cut to the convent. Six words there,
While I stood munching my first bread that month:
'So, boy, you're minded', quoth the good fat father
Wiping his own mouth, 'twas refection-time,—
'To quit this very miserable world?
'Will you renounce' . . . 'the mouthful of bread?' thought I;
By no means! Brief, they made a monk of me;
I did renounce the world, its pride and greed,
Palace, farm, villa, shop and banking-house,
Trash, such as these poor devils of Medici
Have given their hearts to—all at eight years old.

This passage deserves more detailed examination than it is possible to give here. The verse is blank verse, ten-syllabled lines in iambic pentameter. The number of syllables is regular, but stress and the positioning of the caesura are varied with considerable subtlety. In the first two lines one notices the pathos which is created by the matter-of-fact statement of the death of his parents; the stress falls on the 'And' at the beginning of the second line, giving a cumulative effect; the fact that the first line has no caesura and runs on into the second, the only pause being on the 'And', makes the pause between 'died' and the next clause stronger and increases the emphasis on the repeated 'died'. The matter-of-fact tone in which the story is being told is increased by the parenthetic detail. Line 3 has two caesuras—

I starved there,/ God knows how,/ a year or two—

—which throws the middle clause into relief; line 9 is a piece of information not directly connected with the course of events, but the very presence of it increases conviction of the authenticity of the report. The lists in the passage serve a very definite purpose. The first—

On fig-skins, melon-parings, rinds and shucks,
Refuse and rubbish.

—provides more 'circumstantial detail' suggesting that the speaker really knows the nature of starvation; the last four objects, with alliteration on the r's and with the concrete suggestiveness of the word 'shucks', help to create this impression. The second list—

Palace, farm, villa, shop and banking-house. . . .

—by its comprehensiveness prepares us for the strength of the statement in the last line and for the surprise with which we greet the appearance of the word which describes them at the beginning of the line which follows—'Trash'.

Similar care is shown in the way in which Browning describes the friar. The stress on food in line 14 and the enjoyment which the friar is taking in his, compare ironically with the child's lack of it, and give the lie to the description in line 15:

Wiping his own mouth, 'twas refection-time—
'To quit this very miserable world?'

The 'very' is out of place in the context; the friar goes too far in his condemnation of what he so obviously enjoys. The same degree of skill is shown in the way in which the speed of the verse is managed throughout. The increasingly fast movement of the last four lines, coming after the relatively stilted movement in the dialogue passage (lines 13–17), comes to a sudden halt at the caesura in the last line, and so gives, as it were, the weight of the whole passage to our realization of the last half line and all that it implies—

. . . all at eight years old.

The zest for life which is implied in the passage shines through the whole of Lippo's monologue. The recurrent refrain which runs through his head—

> *Flower o' the broom,*
> *Take away love, and our earth is a tomb!*
> *Flower o' the quince,*
> *I let Lisa go, and what good in life since?*

—is symptomatic of the extreme vitality which he pours into his painting. From the very first, in his reaction to the faces of the guard around him, Lippo implies what he later states—that Art is the product of Life. The eye that sees the soldier as Judas—

> He's Judas to a tittle, that man is!
> Just such a face!

—that prefers the Prior's niece to the patron saint, is that which searches the beauty of the world, satisfied with it as a reflection of the beauty of God:

> Or say there's beauty with no soul at all—
> (I never saw it—put the case the same)
> If you get simple beauty and nought else,
> You get about the best thing God invents. . . .

> . . . This world's no blot for us,
> Nor blank; it means intensely, and means good:
> To find its meaning is my meat and drink. . . .

The force with which Lippo makes his apology—his argument against Idealism in Art—is the force of his own being; the zest with which he lives and paints, the prime factor in his assertion of principle.

### 'CALIBAN UPON SETEBOS'

The sub-title of this poem—*Natural Theology in the Island*—tells us something about the way in which Browning's mind was working at the time when he was writing it. At this time in his life Browning was preoccupied with religious questions. The middle years of the nineteenth century were a period marked by a fundamental re-organization of religious thought. The popular discovery of the concept of Evolution followed the publication of Charles Darwin's *Origin of Species*, in 1859. The religious atmosphere had already been disturbed by the publication of the works of the Bible critics; in particular, Richard Strauss's *Life of Jesus* (1835), which Browning showed himself aware of when he wrote *Christmas Eve*. The work of the critics was disturbing in that it suggested that the Scriptures were not historically accurate documents and threw doubt on their statements about miracles and the Divinity of Christ. The work of the geologists and biologists proved that *Genesis* at least, could not be taken literally. In 1860 *Essays and Reviews* was published, containing articles by Benjamin Jowett and Mark Pattison among others, which attempted to assimilate into the Church the new ideas. *Dramatis Personae*, the volume that Browning published in 1865, can almost be read as a commentary on this situation. Some of the poems are direct answers to questions of the day. *Mister Sludge the Medium* attacks the spiritualism made popular by Daniel Home (with whom Browning had a personal quarrel); *A Death in the Desert* asserts the authenticity of the Gospel according to St. John, attacked in Ernest Renan's *Life of Christ*, (published in 1863). The *Epilogue* to the volume contains a statement of Browning's position with regard to organized Christianity, based on the sublimation of the spirit of man:

> Why, where's the need of Temple, when the walls
> O' the world are that? What use of swells and falls
> From Levites' choir, Priests' cries, and trumpet-calls?
>
> That one Face, far from vanish, rather grows,
> Or decomposes but to recompose,
> Become my universe that feels and knows.
>
> Epilogue xi, xii

These last lines of the *Epilogue* probably contain Browning's reaction to the ritualistic movement in the Church of England, which placed a new emphasis on the form of worship. *Caliban upon Setebos* takes up the question of Natural Theology, and examines its tenets in the light of evolutionary knowledge.

Natural Theology is that study which claims to discover the characteristics of the Creator in the characteristics of the Creation. It is distinct from theology based on revelation, or the information which God himself has given us in the Scriptures and the lives of the saints. The argument of Natural Theology is that we can deduce the nature of God from the nature of man and the world. This is what Caliban is doing in the poem. His attempt is an ironic comment on the attempt of nineteenth-century theologians who tried to do the same thing. The Setebos of the title is the God of Caliban's mother, Sycorax; we learn of both in Shakespeare's *The Tempest*, which provided Browning with the setting for his poem:

> This island's mine by Sycorax my mother . . .
>
> I must obey: his art is of such power,
> It would control my dam's god, Setebos,
> And make a vassal of him.
>
> THE TEMPEST I, 2

The epigraph to the poem—

> Thou thoughtest I was altogether such a one as thyself...
>
> Epigraph to CALIBAN UPON SETEBOS

—indicates its subject, which is the attempt of a creature only half human to establish the nature of the Power above him from the evidence which he finds within and without himself. Just as Caliban deduces by Natural Theology a warped and deficient God, so, Browning implies, the Natural Theologian, being merely human, will also deduce an unsatisfactory God.

The method by which this statement is made is dramatic. Caliban's imaginings as to the nature of the Divinity are made concrete and vivid by means of the realization of the creature himself. The fact that he is incapable of properly verbalized rational thought is indicated dramatically in the language Browning gives him; the verbs are either imperative or third person present indicative—suggesting an imperfectly developed consciousness:

> Will sprawl. . . .
> He looks out. . . .
> Thinketh. . . .

On the other hand, the highly developed consciousness of physical things and the animal senses of Caliban come across through the vividness and sharpness with which he talks of the objects around him. The range of Caliban's experience is limited, but his perception within those limitations is extremely keen; his sensuality comes out clearly in the opening lines:

> Will sprawl, now that the heat of day is best,
> Flat on his belly in the pit's much mire,
> With elbows wide, fists clenched to prop his chin.
> And, while he kicks both feet in the cool slush,
> And feels about his spine small eft-things course,
> Run in and out each arm, and make him laugh:
> And while above his head a pompion-plant,

Coating the cave-top as a brow its eye,
Creeps down to touch and tickle hair and beard,
And now a flower drops with a bee inside,
And now a fruit to snap at, catch and crunch. . . .

The creature who is revealing himself in this poem is one who
sees mainly through his senses. The result of his attempt to
discover what God is like is the imagining of a Deity whose
nature is only an extension of his own. Like Caliban, Setebos
has power over things beneath him, but also limitations of that
power. Consequently, he is unable to create a mate for himself
and makes instead weaker beings on whom he can vent his
spite. Caliban imagines that Setebos—

Made all we see, and us, in spite: how else?
He could not, Himself, make a second self
To be His mate; as well have made Himself:
He would not make what he mislikes or slights,
An eyesore to Him, or not worth His pains:
But did, in envy, listlessness or sport,
Make what Himself would fain, in a manner, be—
Weaker in most points, stronger in a few,
Worthy, and yet mere playthings all the while. . . .

Caliban is lonely; he cannot conceive of love; his loneliness and
boredom are the factors which cause him to exercise his power
over other things. Because he cannot conceive of love as a
motivating factor he is left only with the spite which governs
his own actions:

'Thinketh, such shows nor right nor wrong in Him,
Nor kind, nor cruel: He is strong and Lord.
'Am strong myself compared to yonder crabs
That march now from the mountain to the sea;
'Let twenty pass, and stone the twenty-first,
Loving not, hating not, just choosing so.
'Say, the first straggler that boasts purple spots
Shall join the file, one pincer twisted off; . . .
As it likes me each time, I do: so He.

Yet Caliban is almost human. He is capable of reaching past the concept of Setebos to some source of further power which does not possess the individuality which is to both himself and Setebos a source of misery as well as happiness:

> There may be something quiet o'er His head,
> Out of His reach, that feels nor joy nor grief,
> Since both derive from weakness in some way.

Working by analogy with his own reaction to Prospero's superiority, Caliban imagines that it is the very existence of this 'quiet' over Setebos which stimulated the latter to create the world. His whole religion consists in avoiding the punishment which will follow if he shows either happiness or revolt. His only hope is that Setebos will meet the fate which he knows will come to himself—old age and resultant weakness. The basis of his reverence is fear, and it is with a dramatic demonstration of this that the poem ends:

> What, what? A curtain o'er the world at once!
> Crickets stop hissing; not a bird—or, yes,
> There scuds His raven that has told Him all! . . .
> His thunder follows! Fool to jibe at Him!
> Lo! 'Lieth flat and loveth Setebos!
> 'Maketh his teeth meet through his upper lip,
> Will let those quails fly, will not eat this month
> One little mess of whelks, so he may 'scape!

The poem leaves us with a strong impression of the impossibility of Caliban's reaching farther than a perception of his own nature in attempting to define that of his God. By implication, the Natural Theologian can do no more.

Like all the dramatic monologues in *Men and Women* and *Dramatis Personae*, *Caliban upon Setebos* makes its point powerfully but indirectly. A direct statement may be effective if the language in which it is made is sufficiently subtle to generate emotional consent in the reader, but the dramatic monologue has the advantage of involving the statement in a situation which is made real. We accept the statement made in the three monologues considered in this chapter because while we are reading we believe in the characters who speak them and in the situations which are reflected in their speech. These poems are examples of Browning's most mature use of the form before it was given a further function in *The Ring and the Book*. The dramatic monologue can only remain effective so long as it is not too obviously *used* by the poet to put across some moral teaching—so long as he appears to be concerned more with the speaker than with the statement. After *The Ring and the Book*, Browning no longer succeeds in giving this impression. The dramatic monologue as it appears in *Prince Hohenstiel Schwangau* (1871) has become a mannerism rather than a manner. Towards the end of his career Browning did seem to be developing the form in *Parleyings with Certain People of Importance*, but on the whole the monologues written after 1868 lack vividness and power. This was, in a way, an inevitable result of the achievement which is represented by *The Ring and the Book*. In that poem Browning exploited the form which he had developed almost unconsciously up to about 1863 and used it to the full extent of its capacity. After that, there was little that he could do with it except use it again in the same way. The result was a staleness which was only too apparent in the work which was written in the later part of his career.

# 5

# 'The Ring and the Book'

This poem is the longest and the most complex of all Browning's works. It consists of a series of dramatic monologues spoken by characters all concerned in the culmination of a long and complicated story—the trial of Count Guido Franceschini for the murder of his wife, Pompilia Comparini. Browning chooses to deal primarily with a series of situations rather than with the events themselves. Basically the poem is neither dramatic nor narrative. Each of the monologues of which it is composed reveals a different aspect of the central fact, which is the murder itself. The material of the poem Browning obtained from the book which features in its title. In a market square one day in Florence, he discovers what he calls in the poem—

> ... this square old yellow Book, I toss
> I' the air, and catch again, and twirl about
> By the crumpled vellum covers,—pure crude fact
> Secreted from man's life when hearts beat hard,
> And brains, high-blooded, ticked two centuries since. . . .
>
> .33–37

In the opening section (entitled *The Ring and the Book*), and in the closing section (*The Book and the Ring*), he speaks in his own person and explains the title of the poem. In order to do this, he puts forward the metaphor of the Tuscan ring, which is fashioned from a mixture of pure gold and alloy. When the shape of the ring has been made, the craftsman directs a spurt of acid on to the surface; he alloy is dissolved and the gold remains in its purity. Browning says that this process is parallel to that by which he created his poems. He has taken the equivalent of the gold, which is the fact or Truth which lies in the book. With this he has mixed his fancy in order to make it workable, finally withdrawing his own personality in the process of re-creating the tale, leaving pure Truth in the poem:

> Now, as the ingot, ere the ring was forged,
> Lay gold, (beseech you, hold that figure fast!)
> So, in this book lay absolutely truth,
> Fanciless fact . . .
> . . . thence bit by bit I dug
> The lingot truth, that memorable day,
> Assayed and knew my piecemeal gain was gold,—
> Yes; but from something else surpassing that,
> Something of mine which, mixed up with the mass,
> Made it bear hammer and be firm to file.
> Fancy with fact is just one fact the more;
> To-whit, that fancy has informed, transpierced. . . .
> I fused my live soul and that inert-stuff,
> Before attempting smithcraft. . . .
>                 THE RING AND THE BOOK *141–144, 458–470*

The process is the reflection in human terms of the process of Divine creation; it is—

> —Mimic creation, galvanism for life,
> But still a glory portioned in the scale.
>                 THE RING AND THE BOOK *740–741*

The task of the poet, as Browning explains, is the task of all men on a larger scale—the imitation of God according to human capacity.

The process of conception and creation which is outlined in the poem was the work of several years. Browning did not seem to think of the story as the subject matter of a poem until about two years after the time when he found the book. Then, in 1862, he made efforts to obtain all the available accounts of the crime, actually beginning to write the poem in October

1864. Once it was begun, he worked at it regularly for four years, until it was published in four parts between November 1868 and February 1869.

The 'old Yellow Book' which Browning discovered in Florence was entitled—

> A setting-forth of the entire Criminal Cause against *Guido Franceschini*, Nobleman of Arezzo, and his Bravoes, who were put to death in Rome, February 22, 1698. The first by beheading, the other four by the gallows. Roman Murder-Case. In which it is disputed whether and when a Husband may kill his Adulterous wife without incurring the ordinary penalty.

The story which lay behind the trial, the arguments of which are collected in the book, is told in the poem eleven times, each time from a different point of view. In outline, it is as follows.

Pietro and Violante Comparini lived in Rome, moderately well-off by reason of an inherited income which, on the death of Pietro and in default of his having children, would revert to another branch of his family. The beginning of the events which led up to the murder was the pressing of Pietro's creditors for the settlement of debts which they feared his widow would be unable to pay after his death. Violante, in this situation, pretended pregnancy, and passed off the child of a prostitute as her own. The child, christened Pompilia, Pietro innocently accepted as his own and brought up as his daughter and heiress until she was thirteen, a beautiful and innocent girl.

At this stage, Count Guido Franceschini enters the story. The senior member of an ancient Tuscan house, he had been for thirty years the unrewarded follower of a Cardinal. Unlike his brothers Paolo and Girolamo, he had not taken full orders, but was a deacon of the Church. At the age of forty-six, he had decided that no further advancement was possible to him and that the best thing for him to do would be to make an advantageous marriage and retire to the family estates at Arezzo. With the help of Paolo, he discovered Pompilia and succeeded in persuading Violante that the alliance would be a satisfactory one. Pietro, however, was not convinced, so the brothers were forced to persuade Violante to deceive her husband and bring Pompilia, completely unaware of the whole situation, to the Church of St. Lorenzo, where she was secretly married to Guido. Pietro greeted the news of the marriage with anger, but was obliged to accept the *fait accompli* and entered into a marriage settlement which transferred control over all his property to Guido in exchange for board for himself and Violante at Arezzo.

This arrangement did not last long. At Arezzo the Franceschini family, actually in far poorer circumstances than they had pretended, combined to make the lives of the Comparini so uncomfortable that they fled back to Rome, where they entered into a law suit for the restitution of their property. In this situation Violante felt herself obliged to take advantage of the Papal Jubilee to confess her deception. The priest imposed public confession on her. Once the fact that Pompilia was not actually the daughter of the Comparini was made public, Pietro's case for the restitution of his money was strengthened.

Meanwhile, however, the situation of Pompilia at Arezzo was almost unbearable. Guido hated her and desired nothing more than to get rid of her, but he had to do so in a way that would allow him to keep her property. The obvious course was to make her so miserable that she was willing to do anything in order to escape. If she ran away, then he would have the right to keep her property, without keeping her. The most wicked aspect of his treatment of her with this object in mind was his encouragement of his youngest brother, Girolamo, in his attempts to seduce Pompilia. Under such pressure, her life was miserable to her and was made even worse when Guido suddenly insisted on consummating the marriage and made her share his own bed. In order to avoid this she went to the Archbishop of Arezzo for help. He handed her back to Guido. Then, when she found that she was pregnant she suddenly became desperate to escape. She went to the Governor of the city, who treated her as the Archbishop had done. She persuaded a poor Augustine friar to write a letter to her parents asking them for help. He agreed, but thought better of offending those in power, and did not send the letter.

Finally, Pompilia turned for help to the young priest, Caponsacchi. For some time Guido had been attempting, by means of forged letters, to bring the two together, so that he should have reason for a divorce. Pompilia's maid, who was also Guido's mistress, had been employed to carry them to and fro. Caponsacchi, though a priest, was also a young, handsome dilettante, and seemed the obvious target for Guido's designs. Guido, however, took no account of the nobleness of soul of either his wife or Caponsacchi. A meeting between them and Pompilia's plea for rescue brought about a mutual recognition of spiritual nobility and aroused a love which was completely pure. They fled together towards Rome. When only one stage away from their object Pompilia found that she could not go on without resting. They spent the night at an inn, and it was there that Guido caught up with them, sword in hand. He was unable to take the summary vengeance that he might have been planning by the fact that Caponsacchi was armed as well, but he obtained support from the crowd to break into the room where Pompilia was resting. When she saw him she seized his sword to run him through, but was restrained, and, with Caponsacchi, taken before a Roman court.

That court, in spite of the assertions of innocence from both Caponsacchi and Pompilia, found them guilty of too close an intimacy and inflicted nominal punishments on both. Caponsacchi was banished to Civita and Pompilia sent to a convent. The trial satisfied none of the parties involved. Guido retired to Arezzo, where a local court had declared Pompilia and Caponsacchi guilty of adultery, on the grounds of twisted evidence. He left Paolo in Rome to manage affairs for him. After some time, while the legal affairs were still hopelessly tangled, Pompilia received permission to live with Pietro and Violante in a villa in the suburbs of Rome. There her son by Guido was born and named Gaetano. Fearing his father's attempts to seize him, Pompilia hid her son.

Having passed the news of the birth on to his brother, Paolo cunningly disappeared from Rome. Guido now saw his course clear. With an heir, he no longer needed Pompilia to maintain his claim to Pietro's money. Taking four peasants from his estates he went to Rome and spent a week in his brother's villa observing the movements of the Comparini. On the night of New Year's Day, Guido and his four companions went to the villa, their approach muffled by the snow that was falling. Whispering outside the door a message in which the name of Caponsacchi was involved, they awaited the opening of the door and rushed in, stabbing Pietro, Violante and Pompilia to death.

Violante, who opened the door, fell first. Pietro pleaded for time to confess himself and was stabbed as he was speaking. Pompilia fell with twenty-two vicious wounds from the triangular, serrated knives that the murderers were carrying. The old couple were mutilated. To make sure that Pompilia was dead Guido lifted her head by the hair and then fled with his companions, before the arrival of the neighbours who had been awakened by the screams of the old people.

Guido had made one fatal mistake. He had omitted to procure passports for himself and his companions to obtain horses in the papal territory. Weariness overtook them twenty miles from Rome, and before they had reached Tuscan territory they were captured—asleep in a barn!

This is the story as Browning tells it. As he saw it through the involved legal pleading in the 'old Yellow Book', it was an issue of wrong and right. What interested him was the way in which the truth could be distorted in its appearance to the human mind. Consequently, having told the story in outline, he presents the events as seen by various characters at various points in the action which follows the murder. That action is not involved. Pompilia was not dead, but lingered on for four days, able to testify to her own innocence. After putting him to the torture the court heard the evidence of Guido, and of Caponsacchi, and then examined the deposition of Pompilia. It found Guido and his companions guilty of murder and worthy of death. At this point the advocate of Guido pleaded clerical privilege on the grounds that Guido had taken minor orders. So the matter came before the Pope, who, after deliberation, pronounced Guido's connection with the Church to be no obstacle to the course of

the law. After the execution the affair subsided. The Pope
lived long enough to endorse the declaration of the court which
dismissed the plea of the convent to which Pompilia had been
sent, that, as she was guilty, it had a claim to her property. The
affair lived for a while as a subject of discussion and then was
forgotten—as if such an issue of life and death, of Truth and
Falsehood, had never been.

### 'HALF-ROME'

The first of the monologues that make up the body of the poem
is given to a citizen of Rome who is inclined towards Guido.
It is only at the end of his speech that we realize the reason for
his bias; he recommends old-fashioned, violent remedies when
the honour of the husband is in question:

> . . . a matter I commend
> To the notice, during Carnival that's near,
> Of a certain what's-his-name and jackanapes
> Somewhat too civil of eves with lute and song
> About a house here where I keep a wife.
> (You, being his cousin, may go tell him so.)
>
> HALF-ROME *1542–1547*

It is from this point of view that he examines the story, seeing
Guido as the innocent cuckold, fooled into a marriage, deprived
of the dowry by the activities of the Comparini, pathetically
trying to assert his rights against a clever priest and an unscrupulous wife, forced in the end, against his will, to take the
vengeance which an over-indulgent law refused to grant him.

### 'THE OTHER HALF-ROME'

The attitude of this speaker is made clear in the opening lines of
his speech:

> Another day that finds her living yet,
> Little Pompilia, with the patient brow
> And lamentable smile on those poor lips,
> And, under the white hospital-array,

A flower-like body, to frighten at a bruise
You'd think, yet now, stabbed through and through again,
Alive i' the ruins.

THE OTHER HALF-ROME 1–7

Unlike the previous speaker, this one is unmarried and has no
particular sympathy with the concept of masculine honour.
Instead he is attracted by the evident pathos of Pompilia and
her helplessness in the vile situation in which she has been
placed. It is indicative of the difference between the two speakers
that the one sees her in terms of flower and plant—

> The woman who wakes all this rapture leaned
> Flower-like from out her window long enough,
> As much uncomplimented as uncropped
> By comers and goers in Via Vittoria: eh?
> 'Tis just a flower's fate. . . .
> . . . there's anyhow a child
> Of seventeen years, whether a flower or weed,
> Ruined. . . .

THE OTHER HALF-ROME 71–75, 83–85

—while the first speaks of her as bait to catch a fish; as Eve;
as a gilded fly; and as the chick to Caponsacchi's fox—

> The Canon? . . .
>         . . . never dream,
> Though he were fifty times the fox you fear,
> He'd risk his brush for your particular chick,
> When the wide town's his hen-roost!

HALF-ROME 835–840

The first speaker insists on Pompilia's youth in contrast to her
husband's age, on her vigour and activity, especially in the
flight, and on the physical attractions of Caponsacchi, leaving us
to draw our own conclusions.

'TERTIUM QUID'

Of the two former speakers, the second is nearer to the truth,

129

but both present two sides of a case which is yet to be decided on. Whichever side we choose—as we see from the relation between *their* choice and their character—will depend on relative factors such as our own circumstances. There also remains a third alternative, which is deducible from the opposition between the first two speakers—that the whole matter is a mixture of good and evil which it is impossible to unravel. This is the verdict of Tertium Quid, the third and 'impartial' party. This person is depicted as a member of the Roman aristocracy. From the heights of refinement he examines the sordid actions of his social inferiors and pronounces on them in the spirit of relativity. As he speaks, at a Roman party, to 'Cardinal this, His Eminence that', we see his care to point out the right and wrong on both sides. He takes especial care to inform us of the reward received by the officer of the troop which arrested the murderers:

> The only one i' the world that suffered aught
> By the whole night's toil and trouble, flight and chase,
> Was just the officer who took them, Head
> O' the Public Force,—Patrizi, zealous soul,
> Who, having duty to sustain the flesh,
> Got heated, caught a fever and so died:
> A warning to the over-vigilant,
> —Virtue in a chafe should change her linen quick,
> Lest pleurisy get start of providence.
>
> TERTIUM QUID *1405–1413*

This is a man to whom definite conviction is impossible. He can only plead the relativity of the whole affair as a partial extenuation for Guido, the nobly impulsive, the bull-like, because he belongs to the same social world as himself.

### 'COUNT GUIDO FRANCESCHINI'

This first monologue of Guido's consists of his plea to the court in extenuation of his action; it is a piece of cunning policy from beginning to end. He bases his case on an emotional appeal to the judges, referring to their common nobility and

130

the degree to which he has suffered already in undergoing the torture:

> . . . aie, aie, aie,
> Not your fault, sweet Sir! Come, you take to heart
> An ordinary matter, Law is law.
> Noblemen were exempt, the vulgar thought,
> From racking, but, since law thinks otherwise,
> I have been put to the rack: all's over now,
> And neither wrist—what men style, out of joint:
> If any harm be, 'tis the shoulder-blade,
> The left one, that seems wrong i' the socket,—Sirs,
> Such could not happen, I was quick to faint,
> Being past my prime of life, and out of health.
>
> COUNT GUIDO FRANCESCHINI *9–19*

Guido, as he paints himself, is the picture of injured innocence. He pleads his service to the Church, which went for so long unrewarded, his patience under the suffering inflicted on him by the Comparini, his appeal to and reliance on the Law which failed him, while it recognized the guilt of Pompilia and Caponsacchi. Now he appeals to the Law once more to right him at the end of all and justify him for taking it into his own hands and acting out its spirit.

### 'GUISEPPE CAPONSACCHI'

The dominant note of Caponsacchi's speech is indignation. He has returned from Civita to Rome to give account of his relations with Pompilia a second time. He tells the story clearly; how Guido attempted to lure him towards Pompilia; he speaks of his own youth and the idealism repressed by cynical superiors. Above all, throughout his speech, he insists on the innocence of the relationship. He tells of how his latent idealism and desire to serve God truly burst forth at the sight of Pompilia; of how she appeared to him as Truth itself. He waited for her arrival on the night of the flight—

> . . . —till, at last,
> When the ecstatic minute must bring birth,

Began a whiteness in the distance, waxed
Whiter and whiter, near grew and more near,
Till it was she: there did Pompilia come:
The white I saw shine through her was her soul's,
Certainly, for the body was one black,
Black from head down to foot.

GUISEPPE CAPONSACCHI *1137–1144*

Caponsacchi emerges as a man of powerful emotions and with a great capacity for reverence. All the power of his personality is turned against his judges as he reminds them of how he stood in front of them on the earlier occasion and said then what he is saying now. Hearing his indignation we begin to see for the first time the depth and importance of the issues which are involved, issues which he alone so far has put forward in all their clarity. But it is not with indignation that he ends his speech; as it closes he descends from the emotional power of his denunciation of wrong to make a review of his own circumstances and the life which he now has to live:

I do but play with an imagined life
Of who, unfettered by a vow, unblessed
By the higher call,—since you will have it so,—
Leads it companioned by the woman there.
To live, and see her learn, and learn by her,
Out of the low obscure and petty world—
Or only see one purpose and one will
Evolve themselves i' the world, change wrong to right:
To have to do with nothing but the true,
The good, the eternal. . . .

GUISEPPE CAPONSACCHI *2081–2090*

But Pompilia 'will be presently with God'; the last words are a cry of deep emotion—the cry of a man who has seen his vision and lost it:

O great, just, good God! Miserable me!                    *2105*

'POMPILIA'
To Pompilia, Browning gives a significant statement. In ex-

132

plaining her reaction to Guido, the 'cavalier' whom Violante
has brought for her, she says:

> (Tisbe had told me that the slim young man
> With wings at head, and wings at feet, and sword
> Threatening a monster, in our tapestry,
> Would eat a girl else,—was a cavalier)
> When he proved Guido Franceschini. . . .
>
> POMPILIA *390–394*

The naïveté which needs to be informed in such a way is a
part of Pompilia's character to which Browning gives most
stress. The simple piety which leads her to name her son Gaetano,
after a new saint, in the hope that he will be able to afford more
protection than her five worn-out saints have afforded to her,
allows her little real understanding of what has happened to her.
Pompilia sees things simply; it takes the urgency of her pregnancy to force her to act; and it is in the desperation which
results that her true 'cavalier', true Perseus, comes to her.
Canon Conti, cousin of Guido and friend of Caponsacchi, had
named the latter Saint George—as does Browning in *The Ring
and the Book* (the opening section of the poem). This is what he
becomes for Pompilia. Just as he thinks of her as a manifestation
of God's Truth, so she sees him as the light that shines through
the darkness in which Guido has enveloped her. In the pathos
of her seventeen years, in her fearful ignorance of what evil is,
Pompilia found Truth:

> . . . Through such souls alone
> God stooping shows sufficient of his light
> For us i' the dark to rise by. And I rise.
>
> POMPILIA *1843–1845*

'DOMINUS HYACINTHUS DE ARCHANGELIS'—'JURIS
DOCTOR JOHANNES-BAPTISTA BOTTINIUS'—ETC.

The two monologues which follow that of Pompilia are given
to the lawyers conducting the defence and prosecution. The
first, Dominus Hyacinthus, is depicted as preparing his brief in
defence of Guido, his mind distracted by the thought of the
coming birthday feast of his eight-year-old son. The second,

Bottinius, reads his finished plea alone to himself, glorying in the pomp of the imaginary occasion and the magnificence of his own rhetoric. The speeches of both lawyers are of basic importance in Browning's conception of the poem. They are important because, in their different ways, the advocates are completely impervious to the moral issues involved in the case which concerns them so nearly. Both speakers indicate the essential inaccuracy of human judgment when faced with an issue of truth and falsehood, by their studied legality, their citation of irrelevant legal precedents, their flattery and vanity, and their persistent substitution of the legal issue for the moral.

### THE POPE

This, the central monologue of the poem, consists of the deliberations of the ageing Pope, Antonio Pignatelli of Naples, humble, conscious of his nearness to death and his Maker, called upon to act for God in an issue involving human action. The speech of the Pope is perhaps Browning's most effective statement of the case for the absolute value of truth—the statement against relativity, the absorption with which he saw as the fault of his age. To Browning as to many of his contemporaries, the nineteenth century, with its rampant materialism, was an age which made faith and things of the spirit more difficult than ever before. Developments in science and rationalistic philosophy attacked traditional beliefs in spiritual values which had previously been taken for granted. The Pope makes a direct attempt to answer doubts of the existence of spiritual truth which are based on the belief that all human perception and judgment is relative.

The Pope reviews the past history of his office; looking there for some evidence of infallible judgment, he casts his mind over the quarrel about the sanctity of Pope Formosus, reviled by his successor Stephen, re-instated by *his* successors, Romanus and John, reviled again by Sergius; he asks himself—

> Which of the judgments was infallible?
> Which of my predecessors spoke for God?
>
> <div align="right">THE POPE <i>150–151</i></div>

There is no help to be found in the sanctity of his office, although he knows that the truth is somewhere to be discovered:

> Truth, nowhere, lies yet everywhere in these—
> Not absolutely in a portion, yet
> Evolvable from the whole: evolved at last
> Painfully, held tenaciously by me.
>
> *228–231*

The individual must judge according to his own honest perception, knowing that God will judge him according to the intention, according to the seed of the act rather than to the act itself:

> . . . Some surmise,
> Perchance, that since man's wit is fallible,
> Mine may fail here? Suppose it so,—what then? . . .
>
> For I am ware it is the seed of act,
> God holds appraising in His hollow palm,
> Not act grown great thence on the world below. . . .
>
> *236–238, 271–273*

With this conviction he reviews his reasons for deciding that Guido is guilty and must die.

To the situation which he is examining, the Pope applies the same standards that he applies to himself—he asks what was the motivation of Guido's action? The answer condemns him. With all the advantages of noble birth and proximity to the Church (the Pope says)—

> . . . I find this black mark impinge the man,
> That he believes in just the vile of life.
> Low instinct, base pretension, are these truth?
>
> *510–512*

Unlike Pompilia and Caponsacchi, who recognized Divine Truth by means of each other, Guido ignored the task which God imposes on man. The Pope sees Guido as the slug, the butcher and the wolf, but Pompilia appears to him in the whiteness which is the counterpart to her husband's blackness and as the flower growing from a dung heap:

> First of the first,
> Such I pronounce Pompilia, then as now
> Perfect in whiteness. . . .
> My flower,
> My rose, I gather for the breast of God . . .
>
> *1003–1005, 1045–1046*

His judgment of Caponsacchi is more moderate. Caponsacchi was a priest and did not act with priestly dignity and discretion. On the other hand, when those who should have acted failed to do so, he appeared, the athlete of God, the chivalric hero:

> When the first moan broke from the martyr-maid
> At that uncaging of the beasts,—made bare
> My athlete on the instant, gave such good
> Great undisguised leap over post and pale
> Right into the mid-cirque, free fighting-place.
>
> . . . Ay, such championship
> Of God at first blush, such prompt cheery thud
> Of glove on ground that answers ringingly
> The challenge of the false knight,—watch we long,
> And wait we vainly for its gallant like
> From those appointed to the service. . . .
>
> *1138–1143, 1155–1160*

The Pope's assessment of the situation includes a re-statement of the essential principles that Browning held concerning the relationship between God and Man. His words describing the meaning of the story provide us, in their context, with Browning's reason for being attracted to the subject:

> What lacks, then, of perfection fit for God
> But just the instance which this tale supplies
> Of love without a limit?
>
> *1366–1368*

136

But like his creator, the Pope does not rest content with the simple statement; he tests his opinions against the possibilities of doubt and scepticism, reviewing the sordid world of modern Christianity which displays a puzzling division between faith and action, as represented in the complete truth which the Church offers and the behaviour of its members. He imagines the charge which a pagan, born before the coming of Christ, would make against the world which had the advantage of the Revelation. Such a person, like Euripides, to whom the Pope in his musing gives speech, would, by the comparative purity of his life, suggest that the absolute standard of Divine Truth on which the Pope bases his assessment of the case before him, is an improper standard—one which mankind has no right to adopt.

The Pope's answer to his own self-questioning is based on his perception that, far from being easier, faith is harder in the modern world. Now that Christ has lived and died, men have become used to the truth. Now that the old heroism of the martyrs has become unnecessary, any heroism is more difficult. And in the midst of his considerations the Pope perceives, in the complexity before him, the possibility of a new age of doubt following the certainty of the Church—an age in which the immediacy of faith being lost (dead with him), man will be faced with the possibility of acting directly according to his own nature rather than to the law of the Church. Caponsacchi and the Abate Paolo have both done this—the one following his higher nature, the other his lower. It is against this latter tendency that the Pope makes his last assertion. Guido is judged guilty of death by the old law of the Church, but also by the new law which the Pope perceives. As the representative of the old order, he will assert the spiritual standards which must hold good in the new.

> '*Quis pro Domino?*
> 'Who is upon the Lord's side?' asked the Count.
> I, who write—
>             'On receipt of this command,

'Acquaint Count Guido and his fellows four,
'They die tomorrow . . .'

*2099–2104*

'GUIDO'

The change of appellation which is indicated in the second
monologue of Guido's, and the last of the poem, is important.
*Count* Guido of the first monologue has become simply Guido—
the man's real nature is revealed. His violence and malice show
forth clearly. The pretence of his own innocence is dropped,
and with it the suggestion that Pompilia was anything but
innocent. Guido admits and revels in his guilt. As he speaks to
the two former friends who come to pray with him before his
death, he reveals his total lack of faith, his choice of his own
immediate pleasure in a world in which faith remained a possibility, but was not a certainty. Guido is resentful because he
has acted as he thought the world allowed him to act—he left
out of account such a clear recognition of God as was possessed
by the Pope:

Why do things change? Wherefore is Rome un-Romed?

GUIDO *265*

In desperation and spite at the Pope, he casts off his garb of
innocence:

There, let my sheepskin-garb, a curse on't, go,—
Leave my teeth free if I must show my shag!

*443–444*

He agrees that he has broken the law of the world and is being
punished accordingly, but refuses repentance on the grounds
that there is no possibility of recognizing the Divine in life.
Everywhere the spiritual value takes second place to the materia-
listic, and all he has done is to follow openly what everyone else
does in secret. Having followed out the law of his own nature—
the nature for which he is not responsible—he can conceive of
no eternal punishment—

Only, be sure, no punishment, no pain
Childish, preposterous, impossible,
But some such fate as Ovid could foresee,— ...
The strong become a wolf for evermore!
Change that Pompilia to a puny stream
Fit to reflect the daisies on its bank!
Let me turn wolf, be whole, and sate, for once,—
Wallow in what is now a wolfishness
Coerced too much by the humanity
That's half of me as well!

*2046–2048, 2051–2057*

After one final appeal to his attendants to intercede for him, Guido fixes himself in this position. Finding his death inevitable, he determines to die as he has lived, defying the hypocrisy which claims to recognize the shadow of God in the world.

But Guido does not die like this. At the last moment he hears the approach of the monks who are coming to take him to his death, and his human nature re-asserts itself, not merely in a frenzied appeal to the two watchers, but finally in a moving recognition of the very qualities to which his life has attempted to give the lie:

Hold me from them! I am yours,
I am the Granduke's—no, I am the Pope's!
Abate,—Cardinal,—Christ,—Maria,—God, ...
Pompilia, will you let them murder me?

*2422–2425*

This sudden and dramatic reversal of the whole trend of the speech forcefully makes Browning's point about the essential relationship of the human and the Divine. It is not even to God that Guido makes his final appeal, but to the murdered Pompilia, who shows in her patient suffering that very perception of God in life that Guido most strenuously rejects. It also provides an example of the way in which the statement which Browning is making in *The Ring and the Book* is tied down to concrete fact—the fact of character.

An account as brief as the above cannot pretend to represent any more than the framework of the poem—if that! It suggests a little of the complexity which Browning obtains by using the dramatic monologue and creating in such concrete terms the human beings who are reacting to the situation. Nor can such an account give any idea of the complex system of imagery with which Browning binds the separate parts into a whole, and asserts throughout the whole the idea of truth which is implied through character representation. Several ideas and images recur throughout the poem. The first of these is indicated by the various references to Molinism. Miguel Molinos (1628–96) was a Spanish mystic, author of *The Spiritual Guide* and originator of the Quietist heresy to which his name was given. Molinos advocated a kind of contemplation which involved the renunciation of the body in an attempt to bring the soul into contact with God. The result of concentration on this kind of contemplation was to place less emphasis on action as part of the Christian life. He was condemned by the Inquisition in 1687, before the date of the events described in the poem, but the degree to which Browning was aware of the topicality of the subject of Molinism at the time with which he was dealing is indicated by his making one of the correspondents in *The Book and the Ring* refer to the condemnation of Fénélon, the main advocate of Quietism in France, whom Innocent XII was persuaded to condemn in 1699. The subject is referred to so many times throughout the poem that it becomes a kind of touchstone. As such, it is appropriate precisely because it encourages the separation of action and contemplation which amounted in the popular estimation to a suggestion that behaviour was irrelevant in judging a Christian. In a way Molinism was a forerunner of Protestantism, which tended to remove the emphasis in Christianity from external acts, to internal nature. The heresy is thus particularly useful in indicating the position of the individual with regard to truth. The Pope alone perceives the grain of truth in Molinism; the other characters only refer to it for their own ends.

> Must we deny,—do they, these Molinists,
> At peril of their body and their soul,—

Recognized truths, obedient to some truth
Unrecognized yet, but perceptible?—

THE POPE *1868–1871*

It is the Pope also who establishes certainty with regard to
our reading of the system of imagery which runs throughout
the whole poem. Throughout, there is a basic use by Browning
in the first and last sections, and by all the speakers, of light and
dark, white and black, with occasional reference to blue and red,
in order to denote moral quality. This is closely related to the
animal imagery. Pompilia is at various times and to various
speakers, a gilded fly; a snake; a fawn; a heifer; a scorpion;
vermin; and also a plague spot, and a lily. Particular stress
is laid on the sheep/wolf relationship and the related idea
of the heifer/butcher relationship. All the characters play with
the basic ideas of the sheep and the Shepherd, the wolf in sheep's
clothing and the difficulty in distinguishing between sheep and
goats. An extension of this is the widely-referred-to idea of the
lamb as innocence, the sacrificial victim, and a symbol of
Christ.

This imagery all comes together to take its final form in the
speech of the Pope. The way in which the imagery is twisted by
the supporters of materialism is revealed when he establishes
the final pattern, which, in the end, even Guido is forced to
accept. Even when Guido is distorting the reference of the
images, the truth is perceptible. Expressing his resentment at
the Pope's refusal to save him, he says:

And now what does this Vicar of the Lord,
Shepherd o' the flock,—one of whose charge bleats sore
For crook's help from the quag wherein it drowns?
Law suffers him put forth the crumpled end,—
His pleasure is to turn staff, use the point,
And thrust the shuddering sheep he calls a wolf,
Back and back, down and down to where hell gapes!

GUIDO *400–406*

If we do not remember the Pope's almost parallel statement when he is speaking of the Tuscan Archbishop who should have been a shepherd to Pompilia, there is enough in this passage to make us doubt Guido's application. The way in which the apparently objective image gives way to the force of his own emotional preoccupation reveals the fact that it is not truly objective. The figure begins with a quag—a natural, concrete image—it ends when the quag becomes hell, which Guido knows 'gapes' for him. The Pope's help was so necessary to him because he knew that he *was* a wolf and not the lamb of innocence which, for the moment, he was pretending to be.

The Pope also establishes the reference of the colours, white, black and red, and it is interesting to see that Guido, as he drops pretence, casts off his false reversal of the image reference:

> My lamb-like wife could neither bark nor bite,
> She bleated, bleated, till for pity pure,
> The village roused it, ran with pole and prong
> To the rescue, and behold the wolf's at bay!
>
> GUIDO *2302–2305*

Similarly he accepts the whiteness of Pompilia (related to her lambness) and with it his own redness, which is fixed by the Pope:

> Guido stands honest in the red o' the flame.
>
> THE POPE *881*

In his own speech red becomes more and more prominent, and its reference is indicative of the way in which Browning prepares for the emotional assent of his reader to his own idea of the situation. Guido says of Pompilia that there was no trace of red, or violence, in her nature:

> Be it for good, be it for ill, no run
> O' the red thread through that insignificance!
>
> GUIDO *2072–2073*

In this statement he tacitly accepts the association of himself

142

with the colour which his wife lacks. Yet throughout his speech, with terrible irony, there is a further association. In two passages he makes clear acknowledgment of the primary association of redness with crime and violence:

> [You wish me to say that] on my brow there burned
> Crime out so plainly, intolerably, red, . . .

>           Ay, my friend,
> Easy to say, easy to do,—step right
> Now you've stepped left and stumbled on the thing,
> —The red thing!
>
> GUIDO *502–503, 1453–1456*

But running through his speech is the insistent association of the colour of his own crime with the machine which is to punish it, and his own blood which that machine is to shed. Thus, he speaks of the 'red refuse' of Rome which his blood is to join; in describing the execution machine, Manaia, he says—

> Railed likewise were the steps whereby 't was reached.
> All of it painted red: red, in the midst. . . .

> This kneeling-place was red, red, never fear!

—and again—

> There's no such lovely month in Rome as May—
> May's crescent is no half-moon of red plank. . . .
>
> GUIDO *219–220, 236, 250–251*

Referring to the Pope, he says—

> He execrates my crime,—good!—sees hell yawn
> One inch from the red plank's end which I press. . . .
>
> GUIDO *338–339*

Finally, Manaia becomes 'the red bed', 'the red thing'. The association is ironic. Unconsciously Guido brings together his crime and its punishment as sharing a common nature and thus suggests a terrifying poetic justice. As his speech proceeds, our realization of this association grows and becomes more closely related to the idea of his own humanity, which is suggested in his constant reference to his neck and the softness of flesh which is soon to be invaded by the edge of the blade. He asks his attendants,

> Do you know what teeth you mean to try
> The sharpness of, on this soft neck and throat?
>
> GUIDO *127–128*

He returns again and again to the violence of Manaia:

> Brute force
> Cuts as he comes, breaks in, breaks on, breaks out
> O', the hard and soft of you . . .
> A lithe snake thrids the hedge, makes throb no leaf:
> A heavy ox sets chest to brier and branch,
> Bursts somehow through, and leaves one hideous hole
> Behind him!
>
> GUIDO *316–322*

When the final dramatic reversal comes; when Guido has to recognize his own higher nature of man and repudiate the brutal self which he has clung to, we are prepared emotionally to accept the change. Through his speech, while listening to his defiant mouthing, we feel the growing horror of the destruction of his man's flesh. Guido returns at the end of his speech to the humanity which he had never really left.

# 6

# Conclusion

*The Ring and the Book* ended with a reference to the 'Lyric Love' which Browning took as his emblem earlier in the poem:

A ring without a posy, and that ring mine?

O lyric Love, half-angel and half-bird
And all a wonder and a wild desire,—
Boldest of hearts that ever braved the sun,
Took sanctuary within the holier blue,
And sang a kindred soul out to his face,—
Yet human at the red-ripe of the heart. . . .

THE RING AND THE BOOK 1390–1396

This is Browning's epitaph to his wife. She died in Florence on 29 June 1861, and a period of Browning's life was over. The poet was forty-nine; he had been married for sixteen years, and he had another twenty-eight years to live. The remainder of his life was far from empty. He was to make many new friends and some enemies. He returned to England with his son, twelve years old when his mother died, and concerned himself with the boy's education. He remained in England more or less for the rest of his life, spending only short holidays abroad and writing steadily. In England he moved more and more frequently in society, forming many friendships with women, but thinking of none of them in the same way as he thought of his dead wife. His devotion to her memory was the cause of his quarrel with

Lady Ashburton in 1871. In that year he proposed marriage to Lady Louisa, widow of Baron Ashburton, but made it clear that his motive in doing so was rather the advantage to his son than any very deep affection for her. Lady Louisa took offence—not surprisingly—and relations between them came to an end. There seems to have been no recurrence of the idea of a second marriage. For the rest of his life his relations with his women friends, like that with Miss Anne Egerton Smith, whose sudden death in 1877 occasioned the writing of *La Saisaz*, were completely platonic. On the other hand, a good part of his time was consumed in expressing animosity to those who had annoyed him, such as the poetaster Alfred Austin, who came under savagely humorous attack in *Of Pacchiarotto and How He Worked in Distemper*; and to anyone who tried to delve into the past life of either himself or his wife. Then, answering the questions of the Browning Societies, the first of which was formed in 1881 to promote the study of his work, and replying to the offers of distinctions which were made to him increasingly towards the end of his life, took up a good part of his time. It was a source of frequent wonder to his contemporaries how he could find the time to write so much.

THE LATER WORK

Browning wrote as many volumes of poetry after *The Ring and the Book* as he wrote before. In 1868, when he published it, he was fifty-six. He died at the age of seventy-seven on 12 December 1889, the day of the publication of his last volume, *Asolando, Fancies and Facts*. The volumes which he published in the last nineteen years of his life are set out below, in the order of publication.

1871   *Balaustion's Adventure*
       *Prince Hohenstiel Schwangau*
1872   *Fifine at the Fair*
1873   *Red Cotton Night-Cap Country, or Turf and Towers*
1875   *Aristophanes' Apology*
       *The Inn Album*

In all this work there is nothing of the standard of *The Ring and the Book*. While it is impossible to deal anything like adequately with such an enormous body of work in this context, it is possible to point to certain features of it and perhaps to justify the general critical assessment of it as inferior to the work which led up to *The Ring and The Book*. A brief glimpse at the last volume will indicate the fact that throughout the period there was no change in the basic opinions which Browning had held right from the beginning of his career. There we see, in *Rêverie*:

'In a beginning God
   Made heaven and earth'. Forth flashed
Knowledge: from star to clod
   Man knew things: doubt abashed
Closed its long period.

Knowledge obtained Power praise.
   Had Good been manifest,
Broke out in cloudless blaze,
   Uncheckered as unrepressed,
In all things Good at best—

Then praise—all praise, no blame—
   Had hailed the perfection. No!
As Power's display, the same
   Be Good's—praise forth shall flow
Unisonous in acclaim!

Even as the world its life,
　So have I lived my own—
Power seen with Love at strife,
　That sure, this dimly shown,
—Good rare and evil rife.

Whereof the effect be—faith
　That, some far day, were found
Ripeness in things now rathe,
　Wrong righted, each chain unbound,
Renewal born out of scathe.

Why faith—but to lift the load,
　To leaven the lump, where lies
Mind prostrate through knowledge owed
　To the loveless Power it tries
To withstand, how vain!

RÊVERIE

These are the ideas which lie at the basis of all Browning's poetry, early and late. But it is interesting to see that this passage, so typical in terms of statement, is yet so untypical of the work of the early and the middle years of Browning's career. This passage is dogmatic—and hardly anything more. There is no sign of either the verbal brilliance of the early poems or the dramatic control of the dramatic monologues; luxuriance and discipline are replaced by the staleness which is indicated in the use of the faith/rathe/scathe rhyme. Here Browning is using a word which we know from the context of the passage and from his whole life and writing he considered to refer to a dynamic and vital concept—faith. To rhyme with it he chooses one word which has associations so literary that 'faith' itself is removed from the world of action—

Bring the *rathe* Primrose that forsaken dies. . . .

Milton, LYCIDAS

—and another which is not merely obsolete, but has to be partially distorted in order to make it rhyme at all. Such a disparity as exists between the final consonant group of the first two words and that of the last need not be a fault in a poem, but the disparity must form part of the effect which the poem as a whole achieves. Such a use of rhyme is apparent on any page of Byron's *Don Juan*. In *Don Juan* rhymes like 'Nunez/moon is', and 'this did/assisted', are intended to strengthen the impression of incongruity and humour which is given by the sense of the verse. But here, where the actual effect does not re-inforce the statement, as it does in Byron's poem, it only adds to the general impression of staleness created by the juggling of the abstract words, Knowledge, Power, God, Love, Good, etc. None of these words act as *words* (i.e., as concrete objects in themselves, having power of their own) and as a result, the poem has neither complexity of meaning nor emotional effect.

It would be a gross over-simplification to imply that this is the case with all the poetry written after *The Ring and the Book*. Many of the volumes contain effective poetry, though none create a cumulative impression of power. All the poetry is interesting to any student of Browning—particularly interesting are those passages where he deals with Art, as in the poem on Christopher Smart in *Parleyings with Certain People of Importance*. . . . Yet an examination of that volume, and particularly of the passage in *Francis Furini* where he refers again to the Andromeda picture (this time one painted by Furini himself, and not the painting by Caravaggio which Browning possessed), is suggestive:

> this Andromeda of mine—
> Gaze on the beauty, Art hangs out for sign
> There's finer entertainment underneath.
>
> FRANCIS FURINI

ANDROMEDA—FROM CONCRETE TO ABSTRACT
A consideration of the importance of the Andromeda myth to Browning tells us a good deal about his attitude to life. An examination of the places in which it occurs can suggest something of the development of his career. First came the passage in *Pauline*—

> As she awaits the snake on the wet beach
> By the dark rock and the white wave just breaking
> At her feet; quite naked and alone. . . .

PAULINE

where the poet is concerned to create a *visual* impression. Here there is no movement—the wave is just breaking—and the focus is fixed on the immobile maiden. The reference in *The Ring and the Book* is different:

> Tisbe had told me that the slim young man
> With wings at head, and wings at feet, and sword
> Threatening a monster, in our tapestry,
> Would eat a girl else. . . .

POMPILIA 390–393

Here the concept is being used dramatically. The focus has changed from the maiden to Perseus, who is depicted at the point of striking the monster. It is significant that in the later poem, it is not the picture that we deal with, but the *idea* of the picture. We do not see the situation or even the picture, though we are told that it depicts—

> . . . veritable flesh and blood in awe
> Of just as true a sea-beast. . . .

FRANCIS FURINI

The focus has changed again to the mind of the speaker who is *using* the concrete illustration.

In fact, it is almost true to say that whereas in the earlier work Browning is creating the object and thereby making the statement, in the later work he is too consciously using the object to direct attention to something behind it. The triumph of the dramatic monologue even in *The Ring and the Book* is that at no point does the statement which Browning wishes to make take precedence over the realization of character and situation—it is so even in the monologue of the Pope (see pp. 137–141). In his later career some lessening of his concern to maintain this balance is evident, and it is this which makes the long monologue of Prince Hohenstiel Schwangau less effective than the earlier monologues. Yet here it is necessary to beware of over-simplification. The tendency to be more concerned with the didactic point than with the medium through which it is made is shown again in *Fifine at the Fair*, and in the fact that Browning chose not to dramatize the story which is given to the narrator of *Red Cotton Night-Cap Country*. On the other hand, *Prince Hohenstiel Schwangau* was conceived many years before it was written in 1871, and it is impossible to date too precisely the tendency to become over-didactic.

This tendency was present, if only slightly, from the beginning of his career, as also was the tendency which we see in the later dramatic lyrics towards the over-simple. In a poem like *Ned Bratts*, which appeared in the first volume of *Dramatic Idyls*, we see that Browning had not lost his ability to vary vocabulary and metre according to character. On the other hand, a poem such as *Ivan Ivanovich*, in the same volume, indicates that the basic tendency towards the over-positive, which is shown most clearly in earlier poems like *Count Gismond*, could easily degenerate into a tendency to choose the violent action as the easy way out of an otherwise impossible dilemma. In this context it is interesting to notice the preponderance in the later poems of themes taken from Jewish and Arabic legend and of stories which can be made to bear an appropriate and comprehensive moral tag. The increased interest in classical literature which is shown by the three poems, *Balaustion's Adventure*, *Aristophanes' Apology* and *The Agamemnon of Aeschylus*, stems from a desire to assert the essential function of Art in directing man towards God; but it is significant that when Browning wanted to make that assertion he turned to literature produced at a time and place as far removed from the nineteenth century as possible. The choice of classical literature, as free from the qualifying factors of time and place, is an obvious one, but on the other hand, in *Aristophanes' Apology*, Browning went out of his way to stress the relevance of Euripides to his own time and place. In doing so, he created a monument to his own learning, but forfeited a great deal of immediacy.

It is profoundly significant that almost all Browning's most successful poems depict situations and persons removed from his own present. Apart from those which derive from his interest in the medieval and the Renaissance, those poems like *Waring* and *The Lost Leader* which do deal with contemporaries of the poet (in the one case his friend Domett and in the other Wordsworth) derive a great deal of their effect from the fact that they contain a heightened and idealized atmosphere. The reason for this attraction to the Renaissance and to the medieval are to be found in the opportunities which they provided for suggesting a bursting forth of humanistic values in the former, and a clear statement of the Absolute value in the case of the latter. But it is interesting that those poems like *Red Cotton Night-Cap Country* and *The Inn Album*, in which he is dealing with contemporary situations, are among his most unsuccessful. There is a suggestion in this that the distancing which he obtained by using characters from history and legend was necessary to enable him to maintain the balance between the concrete and the abstract, the demonstrative and the didactic.

Whatever the reason for this, and for the relative failure of the later works (and the reasons I have given must be taken as being far more complex and relative than I have appeared to suggest), several things are obvious in Browning's career. The first of these is that he was a Romantic poet—that he was concerned throughout his career to assert spiritual and imaginative values above those of the society in which he found himself. This determination he shares with many of his contemporaries, and particularly with the prose-writer Thomas Carlyle, with whom he had more than friendship in common. He departed from Carlyle over the matter of the latter's tendency towards pessimism, holding to a Romantic concept of evolution, which has more in common with eighteenth-century theories of perfectibility than with the Darwinism of his own day. He insisted on the relevance of Art to Society, seeing its function as a factor leading to the elevation of man, which was the main purpose of Life. His early work, while he was under the influence of Shelley and, to a lesser extent, the other Romantic poets, shows him struggling towards a form which would enable him to express the value of poetry in modern life. It was only when he moved away from the attempt to express this idea by means of depicting the poet himself, and arrived at a stage when he could objectively demonstrate the importance of the imagination as an essential part of spiritual life, that he was free to create his best work.

BROWNING'S 'STYLE'

It is also significant that most of Browning's best work is dramatic in the sense that it is supposed to be the speech of characters other than the author himself. Browning was rarely at his best when writing in his own person. As his career developed he assumed a style which was aggressively conversational and idiomatic. In his humorous poems, such as *The Pied Piper of Hamelin,* this was often a source of strength, but it often led to a heavy-handedness and obscurity which was a constant source of complaint from the critics. The idea that Browning could not or did not write with complete clarity and simplicity can be proved untrue by the briefest examination of his plays and many of his lyrics. The early poem, *Meeting at Night,* provides an example of the combination of Browning's characteristic tone with great simplicity and effect:

> The grey sea and the long black land;
> And the yellow half-moon large and low;
> And the startled little waves that leap
> In fiery ringlets from their sleep,
> As I gain the cove with pushing prow,
> And quench its speed i' the slushy sand.
> Then a mile of warm sea-scented beach;
> Three fields to cross till a farm appears;
> A tap at the pane, the quick sharp scratch
> And blue spurt of a lighted match,
> And a voice less loud, thro' its joys and fears,
> Than the two hearts beating each to each!

MEETING AT NIGHT

Browning's poetry was criticized by contemporaries because of its lack of 'poetic' qualities of smoothness and prettiness.

153

He makes it hard, uses frequent inversions and elisions, coins new words and uses others which many of his readers would have considered to be too colloquial or striking for use in poetry. In *Meeting at Night* one notices his use of 'i'', 'slushy', and 'spurt'. In other poems these stylistic features are far more marked. In *Of Pacchiarotto*, where he is attempting humour, his style is almost a parody of itself. Many short passages from that poem could be selected in order to illustrate what adverse critics have objected to in Browning's verse; for example:

> Then, cocking (in Scotch phrase) his cap a-gee,
> Right hand disengaged from the doublet
> —Like landlord, in house he had sub-let
> Resuming of guardianship gestion,
> To call tenants' conduct in question—
> Hop, skip, jump, to inside from outside
> Of chamber, he lords, ladies, louts eyed
> With such transformation of visage
> As fitted the censor of this age.
>
> OF PACCHIAROTTO *10*

The insistent colloquialism and jerkiness of the rhythm of this passage, the unusual words 'a-gee' and 'gestion', the feminine rhymes—'doublet/sub-let' and 'outside/louts eyed'—all these devices are intended to create an impression of humour and are legitimately used. There are, however, occasions when the same idiosyncratic devices are used in contexts where they create obscurity or bring about an effect of incongruity. Such an occasion is that in *The Ring and the Book* when Browning is explaining the use of his metaphor; he comments lightheartedly on the relations between himself and the public:

> Such, British Public, ye who like me not,
> (God love you!)—whom I yet have laboured for
> Perchance more careful whoso runs may read
> Than erst when all, it seemed, could read who ran,—
> Perchance more careless whoso reads may praise
> Than late when he who praised and read and wrote
> Was apt to find himself the self-same me. . . .
>
> THE RING AND THE BOOK *1379–1385*

The deliberate repetition in this passage—particularly of the rather unusual word 'Perchance'—combines with the use of 'whoso', 'erst', 'ye', 'Than late', and 'self-same' to make the passage difficult to read. The difficulty is also deliberate, and altogether the tone of the passage with its mixture of conversational directness and difficulty is characteristic of much of Browning's verse. This is not a bad passage, but it is verse rather than poetry—and so is a great part of Browning's work.

However, that passage is no more typical of the best of Browning's work in the dramatic monologues and the narrative and lyrical poems than it is of *The Ring and the Book*. It is fairly true to say that Browning's verse is at its worst when he is speaking in his own voice. In poems like *Karshish* and *Saul* the fact that his immediate purpose is the creation of a situation and a person, seems to have enabled him to avoid the self-consciousness which is shown in inferior poems and to subjugate his undoubtedly brilliant appreciation of verse rhythms and word qualities to the creation of the poem. In Browning's best poetry the reader is unconscious of language in itself and thinks only of what the language is describing or of the person who is using it. Thus, we do not complain that *Karshish* is full of pedantic terminology or that *Fra Lippo Lippi* is rough and irregular, while we do make those complaints about some of Browning's later verse in which the language is not disciplined by a dramatic purpose. Similarly, we can hardly complain about the language of the monologues in *The Ring and the Book*, although we are forced to criticize the verse of the sections in which Browning is addressing us directly.

Many critics have failed to make even this distinction between Browning's dramatic and non-dramatic verse. The same writers have also attacked him in terms which would lead the reader to doubt if he were hearing about the author of *Luria* or *Waring*, both of which are poems almost entirely free from those stylistic features which are said to be characteristic of Browning. Often the reason for these criticisms has been a general hostility to Browning rather than a real feature of his poetry. Browning has probably attracted more of such criticism than any other

Victorian poet because he has always been taken as the main exponent of what has been called 'Victorian optimism'. At the end of the nineteenth century his reputation was at its highest point. The Browning Societies and countless readers who turned to the work of the poet as an expression of the kind of philosophy which they most wanted to be true, made sure that Browning was placed firmly at the head of the forces of late Victorian dogmatism. Because he was in such a prominent position it was natural that he should be taken as representative of all that was over-simple and too authoritarian when the time came for a post-war generation to take stock of the ideas which they had received from their fathers. Consequently, the period after the war of 1914–18 saw a rapid decline in the popularity of Browning's poetry and as rapid an increase in the number of derogatory criticisms. In recent years all the Victorian writers have come in for a certain amount of more favourable examination, and Browning has been among them. Many of his poems have always been read. The dramatic monologues were popular among readers of poetry when the reputation of their creator was at its lowest point. Now critics are beginning to consider the poetry of Browning as poetry—he is beginning to emerge once more as a poet, rather than as a preacher of false doctrine.

IN CONCLUSION

Browning acquired his full stature as a poet in *The Ring and the Book*—in that poem his achievement is of such complexity and depth that we can be in no doubt about his relative status. He combines the ability to create concrete and convincing characters in particular situations with the ability to achieve an overall vision suggestive of great perception and control over his matter. That a style which is as idiosyncratic as Browning's should yet intrude so little upon the consciousness of the reader as it does in that poem is an indication of the greatness of his achievement. In his later life that style became a mannerism, and he lost the ability to submerge his own tone of voice in that of the speaker whom he wished to put before us. The fact that the metaphor which provides the title of *The Ring and the Book* is only partially adequate is indicative of a basic flaw in his thought. In his poetry he tried to make a connection between the imagination which creates poetry and the spirit which moves the individual to imitate God. Browning fails to make the connection completely acceptable—poetry and Scripture are not the same; and it is a fault in his work that it aspires too often to the condition of Scripture. Much of the strength of the poet lies in the fact that words—his raw material—cannot be used with any finality; they persist in keeping a life of their own and will persist in so doing until the poet achieves a consciousness of all his mental and emotional processes. It is significant that on several occasions in his writing Browning complains of the inadequacy of his medium, as does the Pope in *The Ring and the Book*. Such statements indicate an attraction to ideas—or, as Browning himself would have put it, to Truth —rather than to words themselves, which are the medium through which the Truth must be expressed, and in which it is sometimes conceived. But that Browning should have made such statements must be accepted as telling us something about his mind and approach to poetry. In the essay on Shelley he said:

> I would rather consider Shelley's poetry as a sublime fragmentary essay towards a presentment of the correspondency of the universe to Deity, of the natural to the spiritual, and of the actual to the ideal, than I would isolate and separately appraise the worth of many detachable portions which might be acknowledged as utterly perfect in a lower moral point of view, under the mere conditions of art.

In that one phrase 'the mere conditions of art', we probably have the reason why Browning reached the heights of poetic achievement so rarely, and why so much of his vast amount of work remains 'work' rather than poetry. On the other hand what he goes on to say about Shelley—speaking all the time far more about himself—may fairly enough be adapted to describe his own work:

> There is surely enough of the work 'Browning' to be known enduringly among men, . . . as human work may.

# Bibliography

## TEXTS

*Complete Poetical Works of Elizabeth Barrett Browning*, ed. H. Waters (Houghton Mifflin Co., Boston, Mass.).
*The Complete Poetical and Dramatic Works of Robert Browning*, ed. H. E. Scudder (Houghton Mifflin Co., Boston, Mass.).

## BIOGRAPHIES

Ward, M., *Robert Browning and His World* (Holt, Rinehart & Winston Inc., New York).
Griffin, W. H., Minchin, H. C., *The Life of Robert Browning* (3rd ed., Shoe String Press, Hamden, Conn.).
Miller, B., *Robert Browning: A Portrait* (Hillary House, New York, 1952).

## REFERENCE

W. C. DeVane, *A Browning Handbook* (Appleton-Century, New York).
E. Berdoe, *Browning Cyclopedia* (4th ed., Barnes & Noble, New York).

## LETTERS

*The Letters of the Brownings to George Barrett*, eds. P. Landis, R. E. Freeman (Univ. of Illinois, Urbana, Ill.).
*Letters of Robert Browning*, collected by Thomas J. Wise, ed. T. L. Hood (Yale Univ. Press, New Haven, Conn., 1933).
*New Letters of Robert Browning*, ed. W. C. DeVane, K. L. Knickerbocker (Dufour Editions, Chester Springs, Pa.).
*Dearest Isa: Letters to Isabella Blagden*, ed. E. C. MacAleer (Univ. of Texas Press, Austin, Tex.).

CRITICISM

T. Blackburn, *Robert Browning: A Study of his Poetry* (Barnes & Noble, New York).

*Robert Browning: A Collection of Critical Essays,* ed. P. Drew (Houghton Mifflin, Boston, Mass.). (This book is very useful, as it contains some of the best essays that have been written on Browning's poetry, including some by Henry James, George Santayana, and Percy Lubbock.

# Index